THE 10 BEST

WAYS TO DEVELOP YOUR

KILLER INSTINCT

SAMMY FRANCO

Also by Sammy Franco

Cane Fighting
Double End Bag Training
The Heavy Bag Bible
The Widow Maker Compendium
Invincible: Mental Toughness Techniques for Peak Performance
Unleash Hell: A Step-by-Step Guide to Devastating Widow Maker Combinations
Feral Fighting: Advanced Widow Maker Fighting Techniques
The Widow Maker Program: Extreme Self-Defense for Deadly Force Situations
Savage Street Fighting: Tactical Savagery as a Last Resort
Heavy Bag Workout
Heavy Bag Combinations
Heavy Bag Training
The Complete Body Opponent Bag Book
Stand and Deliver: A Street Warrior's Guide to Tactical Combat Stances
Maximum Damage: Hidden Secrets Behind Brutal Fighting Combinations
First Strike: End a Fight in Ten Seconds or Less!
The Bigger They Are, The Harder They Fall
Self-Defense Tips and Tricks
Kubotan Power: Quick & Simple Steps to Mastering the Kubotan Keychain
Gun Safety: For Home Defense and Concealed Carry
Out of the Cage: A Guide to Beating a Mixed Martial Artist on the Street
Warrior Wisdom: Inspiring Ideas from the World's Greatest Warriors
War Machine: How to Transform Yourself Into a Vicious and Deadly Street Fighter
1001 Street Fighting Secrets
When Seconds Count: Self-Defense for the Real World
Killer Instinct: Unarmed Combat for Street Survival
Street Lethal: Unarmed Urban Combat

The 10 Best Ways To Develop Your Killer Instinct (10 Best Series #10)
Copyright © 2017 by Sammy Franco
ISBN: 978-1-941845-47-9
Printed in the United States of America

Published by Contemporary Fighting Arts, LLC.
Visit us Online at: **SammyFranco.com**

For author interviews or publicity information, please send inquiries in care of the publisher.

Contents

"The killer instinct is a dark cloak that you must sometimes wear, even if you don't like the way it fits."

– Sammy Franco

Warning!

The self-defense techniques, tactics, methods, and information described and depicted in this book can be dangerous and could result in serious injury and or death and should not be used or practiced in any way without the guidance of a professional reality based self-defense instructor.

The author, publisher, and distributors of this book disclaim any liability from loss, injury, or damage, personal or otherwise, resulting from the information and procedures in this book. ***This book is for academic study only.***

Before you begin any exercise program, including those suggested in this book, it is important to check with your physician to see if you have any condition that might be aggravated by strenuous exercise.

About this Book

The 10 Best Ways to Develop Your Killer Instinct: Powerful Exercises That Will Unleash Your Inner Beast is a concise guide designed to teach some of the best exercises and techniques to developing a controlled killer instinct.

This unique book also teaches you how to unlock the true power of your mind and unleash this incredible powerful source of power and energy that will help you achieve success in just about any performance activity.

In fact, many of students have successfully used these killer instinct and instrumental aggression techniques in other aspects of their lives including business, sports, fitness, and other performance related activities.

Best of all, the killer instinct is a mental attribute that can be used by just about anyone, young and old, regardless of size or strength or level of experience. Most importantly, you don't need martial arts training to master these simple, practical and effective skills.

The 10 Best Ways to Develop Your Killer Instinct is simple and direct. It doesn't bog you down with dry theories, mind-numbing case studies, confusing jargon, or pointless and long-winded anecdotal stories. Instead, it's written in simple, easily understood language, so you can quickly learn and apply the skills and achieve personal success.

The 10 Best Ways to Develop Your Killer Instinct doesn't pull punches! It's serious material that contains proven training techniques for developing and sharpening this essential mental attribute.

The techniques and exercises featured in this book are based on my 30+ years of research, training and teaching the martial arts and self-defense sciences. They have helped thousands of my students excel and achieve their personal goals, and I'm confident they will help you reach new levels of success.

In this book, you'll also find step-by-step strategies for dealing with the debilitating fear and anxiety often associated with many high-risk situations. By studying and practicing the concepts and principles in this book, you will feel a renewed sense of empowerment, enabling you to live life with greater self-confidence and personal freedom.

From a self-defense perspective, the information and techniques contained herein are dangerous and should only be used to protect yourself or a loved one from the immediate risk of unlawful injury. Remember, the decision to use instrumental aggression and other related aspects of the killer instinct must always be a last resort, after all other means of avoiding violence have been exhausted.

Finally, The 10 Best Ways to Develop Your Killer Instinct is based on my two best-selling books, **Killer Instinct: Unarmed Combat for Street Survival** and **Invincible: Mental Toughness Techniques for the Street, Battlefield and Playing Field.** Therefore, if you want to learn more about this fascinating subject, I suggest taking a look at those books.

Train hard and be safe!

Sammy Franco

Introduction
Contemporary Fighting Arts

The 10 Best Ways to Develop Your Killer Instinct

Exploring Contemporary Fighting Arts

Before diving head first into this book, I'd like to first introduce you to my unique system of fighting, Contemporary Fighting Arts (CFA). I hope it will give you a greater understanding and appreciation of the material covered in this book. And for those of you who are already familiar with CFA, you can skip to the next chapter.

Contemporary Fighting Arts® (CFA), is a state-of-the-art combat system that was introduced to the world in 1983. This sophisticated and practical system of self-defense is designed specifically to provide efficient and effective methods to avoid, defuse, confront, and neutralize both armed and unarmed assailants in a variety of deadly situations and circumstances.

Unlike karate, kung-fu, mixed martial arts and the like, CFA is the first offensive-based American martial art that is specifically designed for the violence that plagues our cruel city streets. CFA dispenses with the extraneous and the impractical and focuses on real-life street fighting.

Every tool, technique and tactic found within the CFA system must meet three essential criteria for fighting: efficiency, effectiveness, and safety. Efficiency means that the techniques permit you to reach your combative objective quickly and economically. Effectiveness means that the elements of the system will produce the desired effect. Finally, Safety means that the combative elements provide the least amount of danger and risk for you - the fighter.

CFA is not about mind-numbing tournaments or senseless competition. It does not require you to waste time and energy practicing forms (katas) or other impractical rituals. There are no theatrical kicks or exotic techniques. Finally, CFA does not adhere blindly to tradition for tradition's sake. Simply put, it is a scientific yet pragmatic approach to staying alive on the streets.

CFA has been taught to people of all walks of life. Some include the U.S. Border Patrol, police officers, deputy sheriffs, security guards, military personnel, private investigators, surgeons, lawyers, college professors, airline pilots, as well as black belts, boxers, and kick boxers. CFA's broad appeal results from its ability to teach people how to really fight.

It's All In The Name!

Before discussing the three components that make up Contemporary Fighting Arts, it is important to understand how CFA acquired its unique name. To begin, the first word, "Contemporary," was selected because it refers to the system's modern, up-to-date orientation. Unlike traditional martial arts, CFA is specifically designed to meet the challenges of our modern world.

The second term, "Fighting," was chosen because it accurately describes the system's combat orientation. After all, why not just call it Contemporary Martial Arts? There are two reasons for this. First, the word "martial" conjures up images of traditional and impractical martial art forms that are antithetical to the system. Second, why dilute a perfectly functional name when the word "fighting" defines the system so succinctly? Contemporary Fighting Arts is about teaching people how to really fight.

Let's look at the last word, "Arts." In the subjective sense, "art" refers to the combat skills that are acquired through arduous study, practice, and observation. The bottom line is that effective street fighting skills will require consistent practice and attention. Take, for example, something as seemingly basic as an elbow strike, which will actually require hundreds of hours of practice to perfect.

The pluralization of the word "Art" reflects CFA's protean instruction. The various components of CFA's training (i.e., firearms training, stick fighting, ground fighting, natural body weapon mastery, and so on) have all truly earned their status as individual art forms and, as such, require years of consistent study and practice to perfect. To acquire a greater understanding of CFA, here is an overview of the system's three vital components: the physical, the mental, and the spiritual.

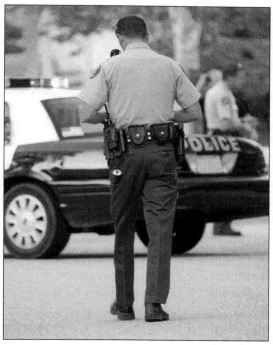

Police officers need practical and effective defensive tactics for dealing with violent street criminals. This is why many law enforcement officers seek out Contemporary Fighting Arts training.

The Physical Component

The physical component of CFA focuses on the physical development of a fighter, including physical fitness, weapon and technique mastery, and self-defense attributes.

Physical Fitness

If you are going to prevail in a street fight, you must be physically fit. It's that simple. In fact, you will never master the tools and skills of combat unless you're in excellent physical shape. On the average, you will have to spend more than an hour a day to achieve maximum fitness.

In CFA physical fitness comprises the following three broad components: cardiorespiratory conditioning, muscular/skeletal conditioning, and proper body composition.

The cardiorespiratory system includes the heart, lungs, and circulatory system, which undergo tremendous stress during the course of a street fight. So you're going to have to run, jog, bike, swim, or skip rope to develop sound cardiorespiratory conditioning. Each aerobic workout should last a minimum of 30 minutes and be performed at least four times per week.

The second component of physical fitness is muscular/skeletal conditioning. In the streets, the strong survive and the rest go to the morgue. To strengthen your bones and muscles to withstand the rigors of a real fight, your program must include progressive resistance (weight training) and calisthenics. You will also need a stretching program designed to loosen up every muscle group. You can't kick, punch, ground fight, or otherwise execute the necessary body mechanics if you're "tight" or inflexible. Stretching on a regular basis will also increase the muscles' range of motion, improve circulation, reduce the possibility of injury, and relieve daily stress.

The final component of physical fitness is proper body composition: simply, the ratio of fat to lean body tissue. Your diet and training regimen will affect your level or percentage of body fat significantly. A sensible and consistent exercise program accompanied by a healthy and balanced diet will facilitate proper body composition. Do not neglect this important aspect of physical fitness.

Weapon and Technique Mastery

You won't stand a chance against a vicious assailant if you don't master the weapons and tools of fighting. In CFA, we teach our students both armed and unarmed methods of combat. Unarmed fighting requires that you master a complete arsenal of natural body weapons and techniques. In conjunction, you must also learn the various stances, hand positioning, footwork, body mechanics, defensive structure, locks, chokes, and various holds. Keep in mind that something as simple as a basic punch will actually require hundreds of hours to perfect.

Range proficiency is another important aspect of weapon and technique mastery. Briefly, range proficiency is the ability to fight effectively in all three ranges of unarmed fighting. Although punching range tools are emphasized in CFA, kicking and grappling ranges cannot be neglected. Our kicking range tools consist of deceptive and powerful low-line kicks. Grappling range tools include head-butts, elbows, knees, foot stomps, biting, tearing, gouging, and crushing tactics.

Although CFA focuses on striking, we also teach our students a myriad of chokes, locks, and holds that can be used in a ground fight. While such grappling range submission techniques are not the most preferred methods of dealing with a ground fighting situation, they must be studied for the following six reasons: (1) level of force - many ground fighting situations do not justify the use of deadly force. In such instances, you must apply various non-lethal submission holds, (2) nature of the beast - in order to escape any choke, lock or hold, you must first know how to apply them yourself, (3) occupational requirement- some professional occupations (police, security, etc.) require that you possess a working knowledge of various submission techniques, (4) subduing a friend or relative - in many cases it is best to restrain and control a friend or relative with a submission hold instead of striking him with a natural body weapon, (5) anatomical orientation - practicing various chokes, locks and holds will help you develop a strong orientation of the human anatomy, and (6) refutation requirement - finally, if you are going to criticize the combative limitations of any submission hold, you better be sure that you can perform it yourself.

Contemporary Fighting Arts is more than a self defense system, its a one-of-a-kind martial arts style geared for real world self defense.

Defensive tools and skills are also taught. Our defensive structure is efficient, uncomplicated, and impenetrable. It provides the fighter maximum protection while allowing complete freedom of choice for acquiring offensive control. Our defensive structure is based on distance, parrying, blocking, evading, mobility, and stance structure.

Simplicity is always the key.

Students are also instructed in specific methods of armed fighting. For example, CFA provides instruction about firearms for personal and household protection. We provide specific guidelines for handgun purchasing, operation, nomenclature, proper caliber, shooting fundamentals, cleaning, and safe storage. Our firearm program also focuses on owner responsibility and the legal ramifications regarding the use of deadly force.

CFA's weapons program also consists of natural body weapons, knives and edged weapons, single and double stick, makeshift weaponry, the side-handle baton, and oleoresin capsicum (OC) spray.

Combat Attributes

Your offensive and defensive tools are useless unless they are used strategically. For any tool or technique to be effective in a real fight, it must be accompanied by specific attributes. Attributes are qualities that enhance a particular tool, technique, or maneuver. Some examples include speed, power, timing, coordination, accuracy, non-telegraphic movement, balance, and target orientation.

CFA also has a wide variety of training drills and methodologies designed to develop and sharpen these combat attributes. For example, our students learn to ground fight while blindfolded, spar with one arm tied down, and fight while handcuffed.

Reality is the key. For example, in class students participate in full-contact exercises against fully padded assailants, and real weapon disarms are rehearsed and analyzed in a variety of dangerous scenarios. Students also train with a large variety of equipment, including heavy bags, double-end bags, uppercut bags, pummel bags, focus mitts, striking shields, mirrors, rattan sticks, foam and plastic bats, kicking pads, knife drones, trigger-sensitive (mock) guns, boxing and digit gloves, full-body armor, and hundreds of different environmental props.

There are more than two hundred unique training methodologies used in Contemporary Fighting Arts. Each one is scientifically designed to prepare students for the hard-core realities of real world combat. There are also three specific training methodologies used to develop and sharpen the fundamental attributes and skills of armed and unarmed fighting, including proficiency training, conditioning training, and street training.

CFA has a several unique military combat training programs. Our mission is to provide today's modern soldier with the knowledge, skills and attitude necessary to survive a wide variety of real world combat scenarios. Our military program is designed to provide the modern soldier with the safest and most effective skills and tactics to control and decentralize armed and unarmed enemies.

Proficiency training can be used for both armed and unarmed skills. When conducted properly, proficiency training develops speed, power, accuracy, non-telegraphic movement, balance, and general psychomotor skill. The training objective is to sharpen one specific body weapon, maneuver, or technique at a time by executing it over and over for a prescribed number of repetitions. Each time the technique or maneuver is executed with "clean" form at various speeds. Movements are also performed with the eyes closed to develop a kinesthetic "feel" for the action. Proficiency training can be accomplished through the use of various types of equipment, including the heavy bag, double-end bag, focus mitts, training knives, real and mock pistols, striking shields, shin and knee guards, foam and plastic bats, mannequin heads, and so on.

Conditioning training develops endurance, fluidity, rhythm, distancing, timing, speed, footwork, and balance. In most cases, this type of training requires the student to deliver a variety of fighting combinations for three- or four-minute rounds separated by 30-second breaks. Like proficiency training, this type of training can also be performed at various speeds. A good workout consists of at least five rounds. Conditioning training can be performed on the bags with full-contact sparring gear, rubber training knives, focus mitts, kicking shields, and shin guards, or against imaginary assailants in shadow fighting.

Conditioning training is not necessarily limited to just three- or four-minute rounds. For example, CFA's ground fighting training can last as long as 30 minutes. The bottom line is that it all depends on what you are training for.

Street training is the final preparation for the real thing. Since many violent altercations are explosive, lasting an average of 20 seconds, you must prepare for this possible scenario. This means delivering explosive and powerful compound attacks with vicious intent for approximately 20 seconds, resting one minute, and then repeating the process.

Street training prepares you for the stress and immediate fatigue of a real fight. It also develops speed, power, explosiveness, target selection and recognition, timing, footwork, pacing, and breath control. You should practice this methodology in different lighting, on different terrains, and in different environmental settings. You can use different types of training equipment as well. For example, you can prepare yourself for multiple assailants by having your training partners attack you with focus mitts from a variety of angles, ranges, and target postures. For 20 seconds, go after them with vicious low-line kicks, powerful punches, and devastating strikes.

When all is said and done, the physical component creates a fighter who is physically fit and armed with a lethal arsenal of tools, techniques, and weapons that can be deployed with destructive results.

The Mental Component

The mental component of CFA focuses on the cerebral aspects of a fighter, developing killer instinct, strategic/tactical awareness, analysis and integration skills, philosophy, and cognitive skills.

The Killer Instinct

Deep within each of us is a cold and deadly primal power known as the "killer instinct." The killer instinct is a vicious combat mentality that surges to your consciousness and turns you into a fierce fighter who is free of fear, anger, and apprehension. If you want to survive the horrifying dynamics of real criminal violence, you must cultivate and utilize this instinctive killer mentality.

There are 14 characteristics of CFA's killer instinct. They are: (1) clear and lucid thinking, (2) heightened situational awareness, (3) adrenaline surge, (4) mobilized body, (5) psychomotor control, (6) absence of distraction, (7) tunnel vision, (8) fearless mind-set, (9) tactical implementation, (10) the lack of emotion, (11) breath control, (12) pseudospeciation, (13) viciousness, and (14) pain tolerance.

Visualization and crisis rehearsal are just two techniques used to develop, refine, and channel this extraordinary source of strength and energy so that it can be used to its full potential.

Strategic/Tactical Awareness

Strategy is the bedrock of preparedness. In CFA, there are three unique categories of strategic awareness that will diminish the likelihood of criminal victimization. They are criminal awareness, situational awareness, and self-awareness. When developed, these essential skills prepare you to assess a wide variety of threats instantaneously and accurately. Once you've made a proper threat assessment, you will be able to choose one of the following five self-defense options: comply, escape, de-escalate, assert, or fight back.

CFA also teaches students to assess a variety of other important factors, including the assailant's demeanor, intent, range, positioning and weapon capability, as well as such environmental issues as escape routes, barriers, terrain, and makeshift weaponry. In addition to assessment skills, CFA also teaches students how to enhance perception and observation skills.

Analysis and Integration Skills

The analytical process is intricately linked to understanding how to defend yourself in any threatening situation. If you want to be the best, every aspect of fighting and personal protection must be dissected. Every strategy, tactic, movement, and concept must be broken down to its atomic parts. The three planes (physical, mental, spiritual) of self-defense must be unified scientifically through arduous practice and constant exploration.

CFA's most advanced practitioners have sound insight and understanding of a wide range of sciences and disciplines. They include human anatomy, kinesiology, criminal justice, sociology, kinesics, proxemics, combat physics, emergency medicine, crisis management, histrionics, police and military science, the psychology of aggression, and the role of archetypes.

CFA's mental component focuses on the cognitive development of a fighter, including strategic/tactical awareness, analysis and integration, cognitive skills, the killer instinct, and philosophy.

Analytical exercises are also a regular part of CFA training. For example, we conduct problem-solving sessions involving particular assailants attacking in defined environments. We move hypothetical attackers through various ranges to provide insight into tactical solutions. We scrutinize different methods of attack for their general utility in combat. We also discuss the legal ramifications of self-defense on a frequent basis.

In addition to problem-solving sessions, students are slowly exposed to concepts of integration and modification. Oral and written examinations are given to measure intellectual accomplishment. Unlike traditional systems, CFA does not use colored belts or sashes to identify the student's level of proficiency.

Philosophy

Philosophical resolution is essential to a fighter's mental confidence and clarity. Anyone learning the art of war must find the ultimate answers to questions concerning the use of violence in defense of himself or others. To advance to the highest levels of combat awareness, you must find clear and lucid answers to such provocative questions as could you take the life of another, what are your fears, who are you, why are you interested in studying Contemporary Fighting Arts, why are you reading this book, and what is good and what is evil? If you haven't begun the quest to

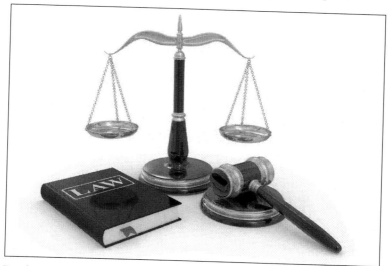

Developing a deadly capability to protect yourself carries tremendous moral and social responsibility. It also involves the risk of civil liability and criminal jeopardy. There is an interesting irony facing most martial artists or self-defense experts. The more highly trained, knowledgeable, and skilled you are in firearms, knives, unarmed combat tactics, martial arts, and other self-defense skills, the higher the standards of care you must follow when protecting yourself and others.

formulate these important questions and answers, then take a break. It's time to figure out just why you want to know the laws and rules of destruction.

Cognitive Combat Skills

Cognitive combat exercises are also important for improving one's fighting skills. CFA uses visualization and crisis rehearsal scenarios to improve general body mechanics, tools and techniques, and maneuvers, as well as tactic selection. Mental clarity, concentration, and emotional control are also developed to enhance one's ability to call upon the controlled killer instinct.

The Spiritual Component

There are many tough fighters out there. In fact, they reside in every town in every country. However, most are nothing more than vicious animals that lack self-mastery. And self-mastery is what separates the true warrior from the eternal novice.

I am not referring to religious precepts or beliefs when I speak of CFA's spiritual component. Unlike most martial arts, CFA does not merge religion into its spiritual aspect. Religion is a very personal and private matter and should never, be incorporated into any fighting system.

CFA's spiritual component is not something that is taught or studied. Rather, it is that which transcends the physical and mental aspects of being and reality. There is a deeper part of each of us that is a tremendous source of truth and accomplishment.

In CFA, the spiritual component is something that is slowly and progressively acquired. During the challenging quest of combat training, one begins to tap the higher qualities of human nature. Those elements of our being that inherently enable us to know right from wrong and good from evil. As we slowly develop this aspect of our total self, we begin to strengthen qualities profoundly important to the "truth." Such qualities are essential to your growth through the mastery of inner peace, the clarity of your "vision," and your recognition of universal truths.

While there are many dedicated individuals who are more than qualified to teach unique philosophical and spiritual components of ancient martial arts, you must realize that such forms of combat can get you killed in a real life self-defense encounter.

One of the goals of my system is to promote virtue and moral responsibility in people who have extreme capacities for physical and mental destructiveness. The spiritual component of fighting is truly the most difficult aspect of personal growth. Yet, unlike the physical component, where the practitioner's abilities will be limited to some degree by genetics and other natural factors, the spiritual component of combat offers unlimited potential for growth and development. In the final analysis, CFA's spiritual component poses the greatest challenges for the student. It is an open-ended plane of unlimited advancement.

The 10 Best Ways to Develop Your Killer Instinct

Chapter One
Before We Begin Our Journey

The 10 Best Ways to Develop Your Killer Instinct

What is the Killer Instinct?

Before launching forward, it's important to give you a clear understanding of the killer instinct and it's applications. Deep within each of us is a cold and deadly primal power known as the "killer instinct." The killer instinct is a vicious combat mentality that surges to your consciousness and turns you into a fierce fighter who is free of fear, anger, and apprehension. If you want to survive the horrifying dynamics of real criminal violence, you must cultivate and utilize this instinctive killer mentality.

Everyone has a killer instinct. It's just the way it is; it's how we're made. In some it may be stronger than in others. Some manifest this instinct in gross abominations. Some never call upon it at all, but it's there. Most people manifest the killer instinct in blind rage and haphazard fury. Self-defense practitioners driven by a raw killer instinct are inferior and undisciplined warriors. Their energies are poisoned by emotion, resulting in poor body mechanics and tactical errors.

The 10 Best Ways to Develop Your Killer Instinct

On the other hand, the person who has tapped into the deep reservoir of emotional calm and mental clarity of the killer instinct can open the gates of deadly destructiveness at will. Guided by virtue and courage, one can release a most destructive energy, free of emotions. This may sound paradoxical and extreme to some. But there is, in fact, no inherent incompatibility. The individual must be virtuous and yet altogether capable of unleashing a controlled explosion of viciousness and brutality.

More to the Killer Instinct Than Meets The Eye

There's a lot more to the killer instinct than meets the eye. In fact, there's over a dozen unique characteristics or components that make up a controlled killer instinct, ranging from clear and lucid thinking to psycho motor control. However, for the purposes of this book, we are going to focus on drills and exercises that place a strong emphasis on *instrumental aggression.*

The Utility of Instrumental Aggression

For many people, the concept of aggression immediately conjures up images of senseless and overt acts of violence directed against another individual. There are others who believe that human aggression is the root of all evil and the primary cause of social conflict and global warfare.

However, "justified" human aggression is a necessary behavior trait that has ensured the survival of our species, and it's directly linked to the killer instinct. Essentially, there are two distinct categories of aggression: instrumental and reactive. Let's take a look at each one.

Instrumental aggression - purposeful and controlled aggressive action designed to help achieve a particular objective or goal. A police officer arresting a criminal suspect or a bouncer physically ejecting a belligerent patron from a bar, are good examples of instrumental aggression.

Reactive aggression - impulsive and emotionally charged aggressive action that is provoked by an external source. For example, a violent road rage incident is a good example of reactive aggression.

The killer instinct regularly requires the application of instrumental aggression. As a matter of fact, I define instrumental aggression as purposeful and controlled violence directed to a specific person while maintaining both strategic and tactical objectives.

Instrumental aggression is particularly important for occupations and activities that require you to administer physical force, such as military service, police work, private security, and self-defense. Full-contact sports like boxing, mixed martial arts, kick boxing, wrestling, football, rugby, lacrosse, roller derby, and ice hockey will also benefit from controlled instrumental aggression.

Instrumental aggression is particularly important for situations that require you to administer physical force, like self-defense.

Setting the Foundation for K.I. Training

While there are many ways to cultivate the killer instinct, I'm going to use some of my martial arts training methodologies to help you develop this incredible source of power. Therefore, you're going to have to learn some combat skills required to perform the killer instinct exercises discussed in the next chapter. They are:

- The Fighting Stance
- Fighting Ranges
- Footwork and Mobility
- Fighting Attributes
- Natural Body Weapons
- Anatomical Targets
- Basic Fighting Techniques

The Fighting Stance

The fighting stance defines your ability to execute both explosive punches and defensive techniques, and it will play a material role in the outcome of any fight. It stresses strategic soundness and simplicity over complexity and style. The fighting stance also facilitates optimum execution of your power punches, while simultaneously protecting your vital targets against quick counter strikes.

The fighting stance is designed around the centerline. The centerline is an imaginary vertical line running through the center of the body, from the top of your head to the bottom of the groin. Most of your vital targets are situated along this line, including the head, throat, solar plexus, and groin. Obviously, you want to avoid directly exposing your centerline to the assailant. To achieve this, position your feet and body at a 45-degree angle from the opponent. This

The right lead fighting stance.   *The left lead fighting stance.*

moves your body targets back and away from direct strikes but leaves you strategically positioned to attack.

How to Assume a Fighting Stance

When assuming your fighting stance, place your feet about shoulder width apart. Keep your knees bent and flexible. Think of your legs as power springs to launch you through the ranges of unarmed combat (kicking, punching, and grappling range).

Mobility is also important, as we'll discuss later. All footwork and strategic movement should be performed on the balls of your feet. Your weight distribution is also an important factor. Since combat is dynamic, your weight distribution will frequently change. However, when stationary, keep 50 percent of your body weight on each leg and always be in control of it.

The hands are aligned one behind the other along your centerline. The lead arm is held high and bent at approximately 90 degrees. The rear arm is kept back by the chin. Arranged this way, the hands not only protect the upper centerline but also allow quick deployment of your body weapons. When holding your guard, do not tighten your shoulder or arm muscles prior to striking. Stay relaxed and loose. Finally, keep your chin slightly angled down. This diminishes target size and reduces the likelihood of a paralyzing blow to your chin or a lethal strike to your throat.

A solid fighting stance must be maintained when executing combat techniques. Pictured here, the author (right) maintains the proper hand guard position during the execution of his kick.

The best method for practicing your fighting stance is in front of a full-length mirror. Place the mirror in an area that allows sufficient room for movement; a garage or basement is perfect. Stand in front of the mirror, far enough away to see your entire body. Stand naturally

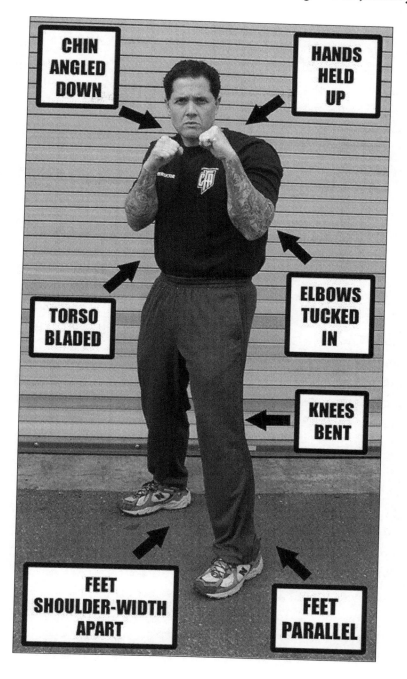

CHIN ANGLED DOWN

HANDS HELD UP

TORSO BLADED

ELBOWS TUCKED IN

KNEES BENT

FEET SHOULDER-WIDTH APART

FEET PARALLEL

with your arms relaxed at your sides. Now close your eyes and quickly assume your fighting stance. Open your eyes and check for flaws. Look for low hand guards, improper foot positioning or body angle, rigid shoulders and knees, etc. Drill this way repeatedly, working from both the right and left side. Practice this until your fighting stance becomes second nature.

Fighting Stance Drill (Shadow Fighting)

Shadow fighting is another exercises you can do to improve your fighting stance. Essentially, shadow fighting is the creative deployment of offensive and defensive tools and maneuvers against imaginary assailants from the reference point of a fighting stance.

Shadow fighting requires intense mental concentration, honest self-analysis, and a deep commitment to improve. For those of you on a tight budget, the good news is that shadow fighting is inexpensive. All you need is a full-length mirror and a place to work out. The mirror is vital. It functions as a critic, your personal instructor. If you're honest, the mirror will be too. It will point out every mistake - poor stance structure, telegraphing, sloppy footwork, poor body mechanics, and even lack of physical conditioning.

Proper shadow fighting develops speed, power, balance, footwork, compound attack skills, sound form, and finesse. It even promotes a better understanding of the ranges of combat. As you progress, you can incorporate light dumbbells into shadow fighting workouts to enhance power and speed. Start off with one to three pounds and gradually work your way up. A weight vest can also be worn to develop powerful footwork, kicks, and knee strikes.

If you want to make your fighting stance instinctual, practice it in a slow and controlled fashion with your eyes closed. Closing your eyes when training will help you develop a complete kinesthetic feel for the movement.

The fighting stance is also used as a reference point when training. Here, a student prepares to throw a kick from a fighting stance position.

When shadow fighting be especially aware of the following:

1. Dropping your hands down.

2. Lifting your chin up.

3. Elbows flaring out to the sides.

4. Tensing your muscles before, during and after technique deployment.

5. Unnecessary widening of your feet.

6. Cross stepping when moving sideways.

7. Failing to maintain a 45-degree angle stance.

8. Excessive weight distribution.

The Fighting Ranges

Real fighting seldom takes place at a predetermined distance. It can also happen anytime and anywhere. If you want to be prepared to handle any type of combat situation, you'd better be range proficient. Range proficiency is the skill and ability to fight your adversary in all three distances of unarmed combat (kicking range, punching range, and grappling range).

This means that you are capable of fighting an opponent in all possible situations. For example, can you fight an assailant on a bus, in a crowded bar? While lying in your bed or sitting in your car? Do you have the skill to strike an assailant standing five feet away from you? These and other questions pertain to range proficiency.

In unarmed combat, there are only three possible distances from which you can engage your opponent: kicking range, punching range, and grappling range.

Let's start with the kicking range.

Kicking Range

At this distance, you are usually too far to make contact with your hands, so you would use your legs to strike your assailant. For self-defense, you should only employ low-line kicks. These are directed to targets below the assailant's waist, such as the groin, thigh, knee joint, and shin. As a result, I teach my students to use kicking range tools like the vertical, push, side, and hook kicks. They are safe, efficient, and destructive.

The Kicking Range.

Punching Range

This is the midrange of unarmed combat. At this distance, you are close enough to the opponent to strike him with your hands. Hand strikes do not require as much room as kicking, and the surface area that you are standing on is not as crucial a concern.

Effective punching range techniques include the following:: finger jabs, palm heels, knife hands, lead straights, rear crosses, horizontal and shovel hooks, uppercuts, and hammer fists.

The Punching Range.

Grappling Range

The third and closest range of unarmed combat is grappling range. At this distance, you are too close to your opponent to kick or execute some hand strikes, so you would use close-quarter tools and techniques to neutralize your adversary.

Grappling range is divided into two different planes: vertical and horizontal. In the vertical plane, you would deliver impact techniques, some of which include elbow and knee strikes, head butts, gouging and crushing tactics, and biting and tearing techniques.

In the horizontal plane, you are ground fighting with your enemy and can deliver all of the previously mentioned techniques, including various submission holds, locks, and chokes.

Chapter One: Before We Begin Our Journey

Pictured here, vertical grappling range.

The grappling range (horizontal plane) of unarmed combat. Also known as ground fighting.

33

Footwork & Mobility

Next are footwork and mobility. I define mobility as the ability to move your body quickly and freely, which is accomplished through basic footwork. The safest footwork involves quick, economical steps performed on the balls of your feet, while you remain relaxed and balanced. Keep in mind that balance is your most important consideration.

Basic footwork can be used for both offensive and defensive purposes, and it is structured around four general directions: forward, backward, right, and left. However, always remember this footwork rule of thumb: Always move the foot closest to the direction you want to go first, and let the other foot follow an equal distance. This prevents cross-stepping, which can cost you your life in a fight.

Basic Footwork Movements

1. Moving forward (advance) - from your fighting stance, first move your front foot forward (approximately 12 inches) and then move your rear foot an equal distance.

2. Moving backward (retreat) - from your fighting stance, first move your rear foot backward (approximately 12 inches) and then move your front foot an equal distance.

3. Moving right (sidestep right) - from your fighting stance, first move your right foot to the right (approximately 12 inches) and then move your left foot an equal distance.

4. Moving left (sidestep left) - from your fighting stance, first move your left foot to the left (approximately 12 inches) and then move your right foot an equal distance.

Practice these four movements for 10 to 15 minutes a day in front of a full-length mirror. In a couple weeks, your footwork should be quick, balanced, and natural.

Circling Right and Left

Strategic circling is an advanced form of footwork where you will use your front leg as a pivot point. This type of movement can also be used defensively to evade an overwhelming assault or to strike the opponent from various strategic angles. Strategic circling can be performed from either a left or right stance.

Circling left (from a left stance) - this means you'll be moving your body around the opponent in a clockwise direction. From a left stance, step 8 to 12 inches to the left with your left foot, then use your left leg as a pivot point and wheel your entire rear leg to the left until the correct stance and positioning is acquired.

Circling right (from a right stance) - from a right stance, step 8 to 12 inches to the right with your right foot, then use your right leg as a pivot point and wheel your entire rear leg to the right until the correct stance and positioning is acquired.

Fighting Attributes

A kick, punch, block, or any fighting technique for that matter is useless unless it is accompanied by certain combative attributes. Attributes are qualities that enhance your particular body weapon or technique.

For example, speed, power, timing, non telegraphic movement, rhythm, coordination, accuracy, balance, and range specificity are just a few self-defense attributes that must be present if any technique or maneuver is to be effective in a high-risk self-defense situation.

Let's explore a few basic attributes necessary for fighting: speed, power, timing, balance, and non telegraphic movement.

Speed

To effectively land any offensive strike you must possess speed. By speed, I am referring to how fast your body weapon moves to its target. A fast technique should be likened to the strike of a snake. It should be felt and not seen by your assailant.

While some athletes are blessed with great speed, you should make every possible attempt to develop your speed to the maximum of your ability. One of the easiest ways of enhancing your speed is to simply relax your body prior to executing your body weapon. For example, when executing a palm heel strike to your assailant's chin, your arm should simply shoot straight out and back to its starting point without muscular tension. This may sound simple, but you'd be amazed how many people have difficulty relaxing—especially when they are under tremendous stress. Another way of developing blinding speed is to practice throwing all of your offensive weapons in the air. Focus on quickly executing and retracting your tool or technique as quickly as you can. If you are persistent and work diligently, you can achieve significant results.

Power

Power refers to the amount of impact force you can generate when striking your target. The power of your natural body weapon is not necessarily predicated on your size and strength. A relatively small person can generate devastating power if he or she combines it with sufficient speed. This explains why someone like Bruce Lee who weighed approximately 130 pounds could hit harder than most 200-pound men. Lee knew how to maximize his impact power through the speed at which he executed his techniques.

Ideally, when attempting to strike your assailant, you want to put your entire body behind your blow. I instruct my students to always aim 3 inches through their chosen target. Torquing your hips and shoulder into your blows will also help generate tremendous power. Remember, in a real self-defense situation, you want to hit your assailant with the power equivalent of a shotgun and not a squirt gun.

Timing

Timing refers to your ability to execute a technique or movement at the optimum moment. There are two types of timing: defensive and offensive. Defensive timing is the time between the assailant's attack and your defensive response to that attack. Offensive timing is the time between your recognition of a target opening and your offensive response to that opening.

Among the best ways of developing both offensive and defensive timing are stick and knife fighting, sparring sessions, double-end bag training, and various focus mitt drills. Mental visualization is also another effective method of enhancing timing. Visualizing various self-defense scenarios that require precise timing is ideal for enhancing your skills.

Balance

Effectively striking your assailant requires substantial follow-through while maintaining your balance. Balance is your ability to maintain equilibrium while stationary or moving. You can maintain perfect balance only through controlling your center of gravity, mastering body mechanics, and proper skeletal alignment.

To develop your sense of balance, perform your body weapons and techniques slowly so you become acquainted with the different weight distributions, body positions, and mechanics of each particular weapon. For example, when executing an elbow strike, keep your head, torso, legs, and feet in proper relation to each other. Be certain to follow through your target, but don't overextend yourself.

Non Telegraphic Movement

The element of surprise is an invaluable tool for self-defense. Successfully landing a blow requires that you do not forewarn your assailant of your intentions. Clenching your teeth, widening your eyes, cocking your fist, and tensing your neck or shoulders are just a few common telegraphic cues that will negate the element of surprise.

One of the best ways to prevent telegraphic movement is to maintain a poker face prior to executing your body weapon or technique. Avoid all facial expressions when faced with a threatening assailant. As mentioned, you can study your techniques and maneuvers in front of a full-length mirror or have a friend videotape you performing your movements. These procedures will assist you in identifying and ultimately eliminating telegraphic movements. Be patient and you'll reach your objective.

Natural Body Weapons for Striking

If you want to be able to apply the different fighting methods discussed in the next chapter, you must have a working knowledge of your natural body weapons. Body weapons are simply the various parts of your body that can be used as weapons to neutralize your opponent.

Actually, you have 14 natural body weapons at your immediate disposal. They are easy to learn and, when properly executed, have the potential to disable, cripple, and even kill an attacker. They include the head, teeth, voice, elbows, fists, palms, fingers and nails, edge of hand, web of the hand, knees, shins, dorsum of the foot, heel of foot, and ball of foot.

Let's start with the head.

Head

When you are fighting in close quarters, your head can be used for butting your assailant's nose. Head butts are ideal when a strong attacker has placed you in a hold where your arms are pinned against your sides. Keep in mind that the head butt can be delivered in four different directions: forward, backward, right side, and left side.

Teeth

The teeth can be used for biting anything on the assailant's body (nose, ears, throat, fingers, etc.). It is important, however, for you to muster the mental determination to bite deep and hard into the assailant's flesh and shake your head vigorously, much like a vicious dog killing his enemy. While this may seem primitive and barbaric, it is essential to your survival.

Although a bite is extremely painful, it also transmits a strong psychological message to your assailant. It lets him know that you, too, can be vicious and are willing to do anything to survive the encounter.

Warning: There is one important concern to biting tactics: you run the risk of contracting AIDS if your attacker is infected and you draw blood while biting him.

Elbows

With very little training, you can learn to use your elbows as devastating self-defense weapons. They are explosive, deceptive, and difficult to stop. By rotating your body into the blow, you can generate tremendous force. You can deliver elbow strikes horizontally, vertically, and diagonally to the assailant's nose, temple, chin, throat, solar plexus, and ribs.

Fists

The fists are used for punching an assailant's temple, nose, chin, throat, solar plexus, ribs, and groin. However, punching with your fists is a true art, requiring considerable time and training to master. Punching techniques include the lead straight, rear cross, hooks, upper cuts, shovel hooks, and hammer fists.

Fingers/Nails

Your fingers and nails can be used for jabbing, gouging, and clawing the opponent's eyes. They can also be used for grabbing, pulling, tearing, and crushing his throat or testicles.

Palms

One alternative to punching with your fists is to strike with the heel of your palm. A palm strike from either one of your hands is very powerful and should always be delivered in an upward, thrusting motion to the assailant's nose or chin.

Edge of the Hand

You can throw the edge of your hand in a whiplike motion to surprise and neutralize your attacker. By whipping your arm horizontally to his nose or throat, you can cause severe injury or death. The edge of your hand can also be thrown vertically or diagonally to the back of the assailant's neck as a finishing blow.

Web of the Hand

The web of your hand can be used to deliver web hand strikes to the opponent's throat. When striking, be certain to keep your hand stiff with your palm facing down.

Knees

When you are fighting the opponent in close-quarter grappling range, your knees can be extremely powerful weapons. You can deliver knee strikes vertically and diagonally to the assailant's thigh and groin, ribs, solar plexus, and face.

Shins

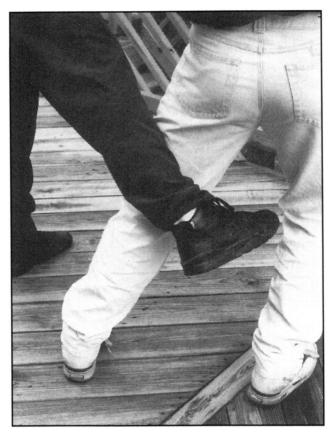

Striking with your shinbone can quickly cripple a powerful assailant and bring him to his knees in agony. That's right—your shinbone is a weapon. When striking with your shin, you can aim for his thigh, the side of his knee, or groin—and always remember to aim through your target.

Dorsum of Foot

You can use the dorsum of your foot to execute a vertical kick to the assailant's groin, and in some cases, his head. Striking with the dorsum increases the power of your kick, prevents broken toes, and also lengthens the surface area of your strike.

Heel of Foot

You can use the heel of your foot to execute a side kick to the opponent's knee or shin. When fighting an attacker in grappling range, you can use the heel of your foot to stomp down on the assailant's instep or toes.

Ball of Foot

You can use the ball of your foot to execute a push kick into the assailant's thigh. You can also snap it quickly into the assailant's shin to loosen a grab from the front. When striking the assailant with the ball of your foot, be certain to pull your toes back to avoid jamming or breaking them.

Anatomical Targets

Knowing how and when to strike your opponent is essential; however knowing where to hit him is equally important. Anyone who is seriously interested in neutralizing a formidable adversary must have a working knowledge and understanding of the body targets on the human anatomy. This is called target orientation.

Many people don't realize that the human body has many structural weaknesses that are especially vulnerable to attack. The human body simply was not designed to take the punishment of strikes and blows. Always keep in mind that regardless of your attacker's size, strength, or state of mind, he will always have vulnerable targets that can be attacked.

Unfortunately, very little information has been written on anatomical targets and the medical implications of self-defense strikes. Every martial artist, self-defense expert, combat specialist, and law enforcement officer has a moral and legal responsibility to know the medical implications of strikes and techniques. It is your responsibility to know which targets will stun, incapacitate, disfigure, cripple, or kill your assailant. Knowledge of the medical implications will also make you a more efficient technician.

I am astonished by some martial art and self-defense instructors who teach ineffective targets. For example, the biceps, collar bone, kidneys, coronal suture, or Achilles tendon are just a few targets that yield poor results when struck. Such anatomical targets won't neutralize a vicious opponent immediately. In many cases, it will only anger him and provoke him to attack with greater viciousness and determination. Therefore, it is essential that you strike targets that will immediately incapacitate the opponent. Anything less can get you severely injured or killed. Don't forget this point.

For practical purposes you only need to know a handful of anatomical targets. We will focus on 13 vulnerable targets categorized into three zones.

The 3 Target Zones

For reasons of clarity, we can categorize both the primary and secondary anatomical targets into one of three possible zones.

Zone 1 (Head region) consists of targets related to your senses. This includes: the eyes, temples, nose, chin, and back of neck.

Zone 2 (Neck, Torso, Groin) consists of targets related to breathing. This includes: the throat, solar plexus, ribs, and testicles.

Zone 3 (Legs, Feet) consists of targets related to mobility. This includes: the thighs, knees, shins, instep, and toes.

The three target zones.

EYES

Eyes sit in the orbital bones of the skull. They are ideal targets for self-defense because they are extremely sensitive and difficult to protect, and striking them requires very little force. The eyes can be poked, scratched, and gouged from a variety of angles. Depending on the force of your strike, it can cause numerous injuries, including watering of the eyes, hemorrhaging, blurred vision, temporary or permanent blindness, severe pain, rupture, shock, and unconsciousness.

NOSE

The nose is made up of a thin bone, cartilage, numerous blood vessels, and many nerves. It is a particularly good target because it stands out from the opponent's face and can be struck from three different directions (up, straight, down). A moderate blow can cause stunning pain, eye-watering, temporary blindness, and hemorrhaging. A powerful strike can result in shock and unconsciousness.

CHIN

In boxing, the chin is considered a "knockout button," responsible for retiring hundreds of boxers. The chin is equally a good target for self-defense. When it is struck at a 45-degree angle, shock is transmitted to the cerebellum and cerebral hemispheres of the brain, resulting in paralysis and immediate unconsciousness. Other possible injuries include broken jaw, concussion, and whiplash to the neck.

TEMPLE

The temple or sphenoid bone is a thin, weak bone located on the side of the skull approximately 1 inch from the eyes. Because of its fragile structure and close proximity to the brain, a powerful strike to this target can be deadly. Other injuries include unconsciousness, hemorrhage, concussion, shock, and coma.

THROAT

The throat is a lethal target because it is only protected by a thin layer of skin. This region consists of the thyroid, hyaline and crocoid cartilage, trachea, and larynx. The trachea, or windpipe, is a cartilaginous tube that measures 4 1/2 inches in length and is approximately 1 inch in diameter. A powerful strike to this target can result in unconsciousness, blood drowning, massive hemorrhaging, air starvation, and death. If the thyroid cartilage is crushed, hemorrhaging will occur, the windpipe will quickly swell shut, resulting in suffocation.

GROIN

Everyone man will agree that the genitals are highly sensitive organs. Even a light strike can be debilitating. A moderate strike to the groin can result in severe pain, nausea, vomiting, shortness of breath, and possible sterility. A powerful blow to the groin can crush the scrotum and testes against the pubic bones, causing shock and unconsciousness.

THIGHS

Many people don't realize that the thighs are also vulnerable targets. A moderate kick to the rectus femoris or vastus lateralis muscles will result in immediate immobility of the leg. An extremely hard kick to the thigh can result in a fracture of the femur, resulting in internal bleeding, severe pain, cramping, and immobility of the broken leg.

BACK OF NECK

The back of the neck consists of the first seven vertebrae of the spinal column. They act as a circuit board for nerve impulses from the brain to the body. The back of the neck is a lethal target because the vertebrae are poorly protected. A very powerful strike to the back of the neck can cause shock, unconsciousness, a broken neck, complete paralysis, coma, and death.

RIBS

There are 12 pair of ribs in the human body. Excluding the eleventh and twelfth ribs, they are long and slender bones that are joined by the vertebral column in the back and the sternum and costal cartilage in the front.

Since there are no eleventh and twelfth ribs (floating ribs) in the front, you should direct your strikes to the ninth and tenth ribs. A moderate strike to the anterior region of the ribs will cause severe pain and shortness of breath. A powerful 45-degree blow could easily break a rib and force it into a lung, resulting in its collapse, internal hemorrhaging, severe pain, air starvation, unconsciousness, and possible death.

SOLAR PLEXUS

The solar plexus is a large collection of nerves situated below the sternum in the upper abdomen. A moderate blow to this area will cause nausea, tremendous pain, and shock, making it difficult for the assailant to breathe. A powerful strike to the solar plexus can result in severe abdominal pain and cramping, air starvation, and shock.

KNEES

The knee connects the femur to the tibia. It is a very weak joint held together by a number of supporting ligaments. When the assailant's leg is locked or fixed and a forceful strike is delivered to the front of the joint, the cruciate ligaments will tear, resulting in excruciating pain, swelling, and immobility.

Located on the front of the knee joint is the patella, which is made of a small, loose piece of bone. The patella is also extremely vulnerable to dislocation by a direct, forceful kick. Severe pain, swelling, and immobility will quickly result.

SHINS

Everyone, at one time or another, has knocked his or her shin bone into the end of a table or bed accidentally and felt the intense pain associated with it. The shin is very sensitive because the bone is only protected by a thin layer of skin. However, a powerful kick delivered to this target can easily fracture it, resulting in nauseating pain, hemorrhaging, and immobility.

FINGERS

The fingers or digits are considered weak and vulnerable targets that can easily be jammed, sprained, broken, torn, and bitten. While a broken finger might not stop an attacker, it will certainly make him release his hold. A broken finger also makes it difficult for the assailant to clench his fist or hold a weapon. When attempting to break an assailant's finger, it's best to grab the pinkie and forcefully tear backward against the knuckle.

TOES/INSTEP

With a powerful stomp of your heel, you can break the small bones of an assailant's toes and or instep, causing severe pain and immobility. Stomping on the toes is an excellent technique for releasing many holds. It should be mentioned, however, that you should avoid an attack to the toes/instep if the attacker is wearing hard leather boots, i.e., combat, hiking, or motorcycle boots.

Basic Fighting Techniques

Kicking

While there are a myriad of kicking techniques in the martial arts world, we are only going to focus on five basic skills. They are:

- **Push kick (from the front and back legs)**
- **Side kick (from the front leg)**
- **Hook kick (from the front and back legs)**

Push Kick (front leg)

1. To perform the kick, begin from a fighting stance.

2. While maintaining your balance, shift your weight onto your back leg and raise your front leg up (your front knee should be bent at approximately 90 degrees).

3. Next, thrust with your hips and drive the ball of your front foot into the target.

4. After contact is made with the target, quickly retract your leg to the starting position. Remember to always keep your hands up when performing kicking techniques.

When performing the push kick be certain to make contact with the ball of your foot and not your toes. Striking the opponent with your toes can easily lead to a severe injury.

Push Kick (back leg)

1. To perform the kick, begin from a fighting stance.

2. While maintaining your balance, push your back foot off the ground and shift your weight to your front leg (your rear knee should be bent at approximately 90 degrees).

3. Next, thrust with your hips and drive the ball of your foot into the target.

4. After contact is made with the target, quickly retract your leg to the starting position. Again, make certain to make contact with the ball of your foot and not your toes.

Pictured here, a push kick delivered from the front leg.

Side Kick (front leg)

1. To perform the kick, begin from a fighting stance.

2. While maintaining your balance, lean back and shift your weight onto your rear leg while simultaneously pivoting your body so your centerline is approximately 90 degrees from the opponent.

3. Raise your front knee up and close to your body (this is called the "chamber" position).

4. Next, use your hips and thrust your front leg forcefully into the target. Contact is made with the heel of your foot.

5. After contact is made with the target, retract your leg to the starting position.

Pictured here, a side kick.

Hook Kick (front leg)

1. To perform the kick, begin from a fighting stance.

2. While maintaining your balance, lean back slightly and shift your weight to your rear leg.

3. Simultaneously raise your front knee up and towards the opponent.

4. Next, quickly twist your front hip and swing your lead leg forcefully into the opponent. Your front knee should be slightly bent when impact is made with the target. Avoid snapping your knee when performing the kick. Contact should be made with either the dorsum of your foot or shin bone.

5. After contact is made with the opponent, bring your leg back to the starting position.

Hook Kick (back leg)

1. To perform the kick, begin from a fighting stance.

2. While maintaining your balance, push off the back foot and shift your weight forward.

3. Next, raise your rear knee up and twist your hips forward as you swing your rear leg forcefully into the opponent.

4. Your rear knee should be slightly bent when impact is made with the target. Avoid snapping your knee when performing the hook kick. Once again, contact should be made with either the dorsum of your foot or shin bone.

5. After contact is made with the target, bring your leg back to the starting position.

The hook kick.

Punching Techniques

In this section, I'm going to teach you four different punching skills that can be used in some of the killer instinct exercises. They are:

- **Lead straight**
- **Rear cross**
- **Hook punch**
- **Uppercut punch**

The Lead Straight Punch

The lead straight is a linear punch thrown from your lead arm, and contact is made with the center knuckle. To execute the technique, perform the following steps.

1. Start off in a fighting stance with both of your hands held up in the guard position. Your fists should be lightly clenched with both of your elbows pointing to the ground.

2. Simultaneously step toward the opponent and twist your front waist and shoulder forward as you snap your front arm into the target.

3. When delivering the punch, remember not to lock out your arm as this will have a "pushing effect" on the target.

4. Quickly retract your arm back to the starting position.

5. One common mistake when throwing the punch is to let it deflect off to the side of the target. Also, keep in mind that lead straight punches can be delivered to the opponent's head or body. Targets for the lead straight include the opponent's nose, chin, and solar plexus.

Pictured here, a lead straight punch.

Rear Cross

The rear cross is considered the heavy artillery of punches and it's thrown from your rear arm. To execute the punch, perform the following steps:

1. Start off in a fighting stance with both of your hands held up in the guard position. Your fists should be lightly clenched with both of your elbows pointing to the ground.

2. Next, quickly twist your rear hips and shoulders forward as you snap your rear arm into the target. Proper waist twisting and weight transfer is of paramount importance to the rear cross. You must shift your weight from your rear foot to your lead leg as you throw the punch.

3. To maximize the impact of the punch, make certain that your fist is positioned horizontally. Avoid overextending the blow or exposing your chin during its execution.

4. Once again, do not lock out your arm when throwing the

punch. Let the power of the blow sink into the target before you retract it back to the starting position.

The rear cross.

Hook Punch

The hook is another devastating punch in your arsenal, yet it's also one of the most difficult to master. This punch can be performed from either your front or rear hand, and it can be delivered to both high or low targets.

1. Start in a fighting stance with your hand guard held up. Both of your elbows should be pointing to the ground, and your fists clenched loosely.

2. Next, quickly and smoothly, raise your elbow up so that your arm is parallel to the ground while simultaneously torquing your shoulder, hip, and foot into the direction of the blow.

3. When delivering the strike, be certain your arm is bent at least ninety degrees and that your wrist and forearm are kept

straight throughout the movement.

4. As you throw the punch, your fist is positioned vertically. The elbow should be locked when contact is made with the target. Remember to simultaneously tighten your fists when impact is made with the target. This action will allow your punch to travel with optimum speed and efficiency, and it will also augment the impact power of your strike.

5. Return to the starting position.

The lead hook punch.

Uppercut Punch

The uppercut is a another powerful punch that can be delivered from both the lead and rear arm. To execute the blow, perform the following steps.

1. Start off in a fighting stance with both of your hands held up in the guard position. Your fists should be lightly clenched with both of your elbows pointing to the ground.

2. Next, drop your shoulder and bend your knees.

3. Quickly, stand up and drive your fist upward and into the target. Your palm should be facing you when contact is made with the target. To avoid any possible injury, always keep your wrists straight.

4. Make certain your punch has a tight arc. Avoid "winding up" the blow. A properly executed uppercut punch should be a tight explosive jolt.

5. Return to the fighting stance.

The lead uppercut punch.

The rear uppercut.

Blocking Techniques

Blocks are defensive techniques designed to intercept your assailant's circular attacks. They are performed by placing a non-vital body part between the opponent's strike and your anatomical body target. There are three primary blocks you need to learn. They are:

- **high block**
- **mid block**
- **elbow block**

High Block

The high block is used to defend against overhead blows. To execute the lead high block, simply raise your lead arm up and extend your forearm out and above your head. Make certain that your hand is open and not clenched. This will increase the surface area of your block and provide a quick counterattack. The mechanics for the lead high block are the same as for the rear high block. Raise your rear arm up and extend your forearm out and above your head.

The high block.

Mid Block

The mid-block is specifically used to defend against circular blows to your head or upper torso. To perform the move, raise either your right or left arm at approximately 90 degrees while simultaneously pronating (rotating) it into the direction of the strike. Make contact with the belly of your forearm at the assailant's wrist or forearm. This movement will provide maximum structural integrity for the blocking tool. Make certain that your hand is held open to increase the surface area of your block. When performing the mid-block, be certain to time the rotation of your arm with the attack. Don't forget that the mid-block has both height (up and down) and width (in and out) fluctuations that are relative to the characteristics of the assailant's blow.

The lead hand mid block.

In this photo, a rear hand mid block.

Elbow Block

The elbow block is used to stop circular blows to your midsection, such as uppercuts, shovel hooks, and hook kicks. To execute the move, drop your elbow and simultaneously twist your body toward your centerline. Be certain to keep your elbow perpendicular to the floor with your hands relaxed and close to your chest. The elbow block can be used on both the right and left sides.

Pictured here, the elbow block.

Parrying Techniques

The parry is a quick, forceful slap that redirects your assailant's linear strike (jabs, lead straights, and rear crosses). There are two general types of parries, horizontal and vertical, and both can be performed with the right and left hands.

Horizontal Parry

To properly execute a horizontal parry from a fighting stance, move your lead hand horizontally across your body to deflect and redirect the assailant's punch. Immediately return to your guard position. Be certain to make contact with the palm of your hand.

Pictured here, a right hand horizontal parry.

Vertical Parry

To execute a vertical parry, from a fighting stance, move your hand vertically down your body to deflect and redirect the assailant's blow. Once again, don't forget to counterattack your opponent. A word of caution, don't parry punches with your finger. The fingers provide no structural integrity, and they can be jammed or broken easily.

The 10 Best Ways to Develop Your Killer Instinct

Chapter Two
The Ten Best Ways to Develop Your Killer Instinct

The 10 Best Ways to Develop Your Killer Instinct

The Killer Instinct Exercises

In this chapter, I'm going to teach you ten of the best ways to develop and refine your killer instinct. Some of these exercises will be mental while other will be physical, but all of them are important. Many of these cognitive exercises can also be used as coping tools during the immediate stress and anxiety of a high-performance situation.

Let's begin with mental visualization and progressively work our way to the physical elements of training.

1. Mental Visualization

Through years of research and training, I found mental visualization to be a fascinating subject. Briefly stated, visualization is the formation of mental images to bring about desired goals ranging anywhere from improved lifestyles and health to better job performance and athletic ability. Established research indicates that mental images cause brain activity identical to that produced by an actual experience. Even if the image is unrealistic or logically impossible, the body will still produce a response that stimulates every cell in the body.

There is no doubt that visualization can significantly improve your killer instinct. To truly reap the benefits, however, you must make certain that your images are clear and strong. In essence, you must feel, taste, smell, and here the visualized scenario.

How to Visualize

Visualization is a natural and relatively simple exercise. The good news is the more often you use it, the easier it becomes. Effective visualization requires a quiet place, free from distractions, for at least twenty minutes. Turn off your cell phone and tell your partner or roommates that you do not wish to be disturbed. It is vital that you have peace and quiet.

Every visualization session must be undertaken in a relaxed state, the preparatory state for visualization. To attain a state of relaxation, you must first sit in a chair or lie on a couch or bed. If sitting, make certain your back is straight, your arms are uncrossed, and your feet are both on the floor. If lying down, place your arms at your side. You may want to put a pillow under your head.

There are various relaxation exercises you can perform. One of the easiest to learn is the tensing – releasing method. To begin, close your eyes and begin to breathe slowly and deeply for approximately two minutes. The next step requires you to tense every muscle in your body all at once. Clench your fists and your feet. Tighten your jaw and facial muscles. Tense your shoulders, chest, back, legs, and buttocks. Hold the tension for approximately ten seconds then in one concentrated effort, let go and allow the tension to flow out of your body.

Killer Instinct Visualization

This visualization scenario is going to focus on developing your killer instinct. Start by visualizing yourself in a dangerous environmental setting, maybe walking through an alley in some seedy part of town. Feel the cool night air rush your body. Envision the gloomy brick buildings that surround you. Smell the rotten garbage as you walk past the overloaded trash cans. Listen to the sound of cars driving in the distance, hear an alley cat cry from hunger.

Now, imagine a distant figure lurking in the shadows, slowly approaching you. Mentally conjure up a person, giving him strong physical characteristics. Make him dangerous and threatening – perhaps a tall and powerful mesomorph. Begin with his facial characteristics and visualize his entire body. Smell the repulsive stench that radiates from his unbathed body. Give this imaginary assailant a criminal motive and a voice to express it. Feel your heart accelerate and your adrenaline soar. Don't forget to visualize essential tactical factors, such as the opponent's range, positioning, weapon capability, and state of mind. Again, it might be necessary to run the scenario several times in your mind to crystallize the confrontation.

Next, visualize an extreme reversal in your mentality – the aggressive side of your temperament. Watch yourself transform into a calm and controlled warrior. You are dangerous, courageous, and free from distractions. Your mind is razor sharp and focused on the confrontation.

Visualize your chest cavity expand as oxygen fills your lungs. Hose like veins protrude from your temple, and your face begins to grin with anticipation. You are ready to fight! You assume a fighting stance, and the storm of destruction begins. See yourself move forward with a brutal and vicious compound attack. The fighting techniques you choose are entirely up to you; however, be certain that they accurately relate to the circumstance, environment, range, and targets presented by the imaginary assailant. During your attack, picture the opponents bone shatter as you deliver powerful blows. Listen to him groan in pain and whimper in agony. Finally, watch the adversary fall to the ground, incapacitated and harmless.

Try visualizing the scenario at different mental speeds. Experiment with different combative scenarios. Change the environment, circumstance, opponent, range, and level of use-of-force. Be creative; remember, no two self-defense altercations are going to be the same.

2. Meditation for the Killer Instinct

Meditation is a technique whereby the practitioner achieves a state of deep physiological and mental repose. It has been used throughout the centuries by the Indian yogis, Taoists, Buddhists, and the mystics to achieve self-enlightenment. It wasn't until the 60s that Westerners recognize the value of meditation for reducing stress, muscle tension, pulse rate, high blood pressure, and other ailments.

Meditation serves several purposes in killer instinct training. It develops both self-discipline and self-awareness. Meditation also enhances concentration. Through its practice, you learn to eliminate both internal and external distractions from your mind.

Believe it or not, meditation also cultivates characteristics of the killer instinct. Through consistent practice, you can acquire

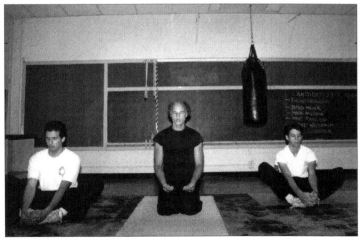

Meditation is vital for developing the killer instinct.

an emotionless state of mind that is essential for high-risk combat operations. Meditation can also be used to clear the warrior's mind after a dangerous and stressful combat event. Stress and anxiety are replaced with inner peace, patience, and a state of well-being.

How to Meditate

Effective meditation requires a quiet environment and freedom from distractions for at least 30 minutes. A quiet and comfortable room will suffice. There is no need to burn incense or decorate your room in an oriental motif. Just keep it plain and simple. Meditation can also be practiced outdoors, as long as the location is quiet and peaceful.

Posture is another important factor. You want to be as comfortable as possible when meditating. There are many different types of meditative postures. The most common is the seated, cross-legged position, where the legs are crossed with the feet under the thighs. The head is balanced and facing forward, the torso is erect, and the hands are placed on the knees. This is by far the most comfortable and unrestricted posture. I do not recommend lying down; you should not be so relaxed that the mind becomes unfocused.

Once you are in a comfortable position, close your eyes and begin to breathe slowly and deeply, in through your nose and out through your mouth. The goal is to relax. The next step is the most difficult. You want to eliminate any thoughts from your mind. The objective is to remain mentally void. Don't let your mind wander or visualize. You want to reach a state of "nothingness." If thoughts or images do enter your mind, don't concentrate on them. Just allow them to drift from your consciousness. Concentrating on "nothing" can be difficult and very frustrating. It becomes easier with constant practice, however. If your schedule permits, meditate every day. If your time is limited, three times a week will suffice. Make sure each session lasts at least twenty minutes.

Remember that results will not come overnight. Like any worthwhile endeavor, meditation requires practice and time.

3. Controlled Breathing

Controlled breathing is a very useful technique for managing the stress and anxiety associated with a variety of high-performance tasks as well as channeling your killer instinct. This form of tactical breathing can be used by warriors, athletes and just about anyone else. However, it's especially helpful for arousal control during high-risk duties such as those found in military, law enforcement, and private security work.

All of us, at one time or another, have experienced the uncontrolled breathing pattern associated with fear or extreme stress. If you recall, it was loud, fast and shallow. Therefore, the objective of controlled breathing is to do the exact opposite. By employing slow and controlled breathing, you will be able to regain control of your emotional state. Deep and steady breathing quickly shifts your mind and body into a more relaxed state, so you can efficiently perform your task or mission during a crisis situation.

How to Control Your Breathing

Initially, controlled breathing should be practiced in a quiet place, free from distractions, for at least 15 minutes. It's best to practice while sitting in a chair or lying on a comfortable couch or bed. If sitting, make certain your back is straight, your arms are uncrossed, and your feet are both on the floor. If lying down, place your arms at your side. You may want to put a pillow under your head.

Next, close your eyes and relax your body. Begin by inhaling deeply and steadily for 4 seconds. Let your lungs fill and expand with air. Hold this for one second and then exhale steadily for 4 seconds. Allow all of the air to expel from your mouth. Repeat this process for a minimum of 15 minutes. Advanced practitioners can also incorporate controlled breathing exercises with mental visualization scenarios. The more you practice controlled breathing, the faster you'll be able to bring about its relaxation response.

Once you master the basics, you can practice controlled breathing during idle times. For example, when you are waiting in a long line or when you are stuck in a traffic jam. However, controlled breathing is best used before, during and after a high-pressure performance situation.

4. Bifurcation Training

Bifurcation training is ideal for improving selective attention and mental concentration when activating your killer instinct. This exercise requires the practitioner to perform a particular physical performance action while simultaneously executing an unrelated mental task. The physical performance could be anything that involves technical skill and movement (i.e., a golf swing, tennis serve, baseball pitch, football forward pass, arrest and control maneuver, target practice, punching combination, etc). The mental task portion of the drill, however, requires you either to solve a mathematical equation or recite a verse or nursery rhyme.

The following bifurcation drills will use a striking combination or "compound attack" as the physical performance action. Let's begin with the pledge drill.

Pledge Drill

This exercise requires that you verbally recite the pledge of allegiance. While you are reciting the pledge your training partner yells, "Go!" and you are to immediately launch a preselected compound attack in the air. The key is to deliver a flurry of full-speed, full-force strikes while continuing to recite the pledge in a calm and controlled manner. It's critical that you do not alter the tone, pitch, volume, or tempo of your voice when delivering your assault.

Nursery Rhyme Drill (beginner level)

This exercise is similar to "the pledge" except that it requires you to verbally recite a simple children's nursery rhyme, such as "Mary Had a Little Lamb" or "Hickory, Dickory, Dock." Once again, while you are reciting the rhyme, your training partner yells, "Go!" and you are to immediately launch a preselected compound attack in the air without disturbing the vocalization of the rhyme. Once again, it's critical not to alter the tonality of your voice when delivering your assault.

Tongue Twister (intermediate level)

The tongue twister is an intermediate-level drill that requires you to slowly and repeatedly recite a tongue twister, such as "She sells seashells on the seashore of Seychelles" or "Peter Piper picked a peck of pickled peppers." While you are reciting this statement, your training partner yells, "Go!" and you must immediately launch a preselected compound attack in the air. Once again, it's critical that you do not disturb the vocalization or alter the tone, pitch, volume, or tempo of your voice when delivering your assault.

The Alphabet Drill (advanced level)

The "alphabet" is a more advanced drill. Your objective here is to slowly recite the alphabet backward. At some point during your recitation, your training partner is to yell, "Go!" and you are to immediately launch a preselected compound attack in the air while continuing to recite the alphabet backward. Don't get frustrated with this exercise; it's designed to challenge you.

Sample Compound Attacks

What follows are five compound attacks that can be employed when conducting bifurcation training. A "compound attack" is the logical sequence of two or more techniques thrown in strategic succession. For example, a lead straight punch followed immediately by a rear cross is considered to be a compound attack. There are infinite fighting combinations you can perform during bifurcation training. (For more information about specific fighting techniques, please see the appendix of this book.)

When executing your compound attack, make certain your strikes are delivered with speed, power, and proper form. You can also perform these combinations in front of a mirror, on the heavy bag or the focus mitts.

- Lead straight-rear cross-lead straight
- Push kick-rear uppercut-lead uppercut-rear hook punch
- Lead straight-rear cross-lead hook punch-rear hook punch
- Hook kick-rear hook punch-lead hook punch-rear uppercut
- Rear hook punch-lead uppercut-rear uppercut-lead hook punch

5. Impact Training

Impact training is another important methodology for developing the pain tolerance component of the killer instinct. Impact training is a series of physical exercises designed to condition your mind and body to withstand the trauma of strikes and blows.

In unarmed combat, there are two types of striking impact: snapping and breaking. Snapping impact shocks the head or body but does not fully penetrate it. It's quick but lacks substantial follow-through. A snapping blow usually makes a brisk, sharp cracking sound when it connects with its target.

In contrast, breaking impact shocks and moves the head or body. It can break or fracture bones easily because it follows through its target (approximately three inches). You must be physically and psychologically prepared to tolerate both types of impact.

Impact training requires both forms of impact to be administered to specific body parts, including the shoulders, back, chest, biceps, triceps, abdominals, thighs, and calves. Striking these targets will not cause severe or permanent injury. Never strike the face, neck, throat, solar plexus, spine, groin, or joints during impact training. These anatomical targets are very sensitive and cannot be conditioned to withstand deliberate impact. Striking these targets can cause severe and permanent injury. It is imperative that your training partner deliver accurate blows and avoid these targets during training.

For impact training, your training partner will need a pair of boxing gloves or focus mitts to deliver the blows. When you begin, have your partner start off slowly with light strikes to your muscle groups, alternating snapping and breaking blows. Always remember to exhale when the blow makes contact. Over time, your partner can increase the speed and force of the strikes. Be patient with each other. It will take time and some experimentation before you and your partner can correctly gauge the amount of power. Impact training sessions should last approximately five minutes and should be conducted at least twice a month.

6. Medicine Ball Training

If you don't have a training partner for impact training or if you want some training variety, you can perform medicine ball work. When used properly, it also promotes proper breathing, physical endurance, and the ability to withstand powerful blows to the body.

One of the best ways to train with the medicine ball is to repeatedly throw it into your stomach while you are lying down on your back. Remember to exhale and flex your abdominal muscles when the ball is forcefully thrown into your body.

A good workout would include a two minute round with one-minute rest period. Depending on your level of conditioning and specific training goals, you might do this for a total of 4 rounds. A word of caution, however, medicine ball training is hard on the body, so practice no more than two times per week.

7. Full-Contact Sparring

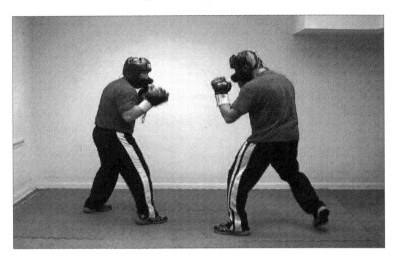

Full-contact sparring is a practical method for developing the instrumental aggression of your killer instinct. It also develops many physical attributes like speed, quickness, coordination, agility, timing, distancing, ambidexterity, endurance, flexibility, tactile sensitivity, pain tolerance, finesse, accuracy, and non-telegraphic movement.

Sparring skills require combining kicks and punches into fluid and logical combinations. Basic sparring sessions are conducted at a moderate and controlled pace. The good news is you can spar just about anywhere, such as a gym, basement, garage and even outdoors. However, before you begin training, you'll need protective head gear, 14 oz boxing gloves, and a mouth piece.

Depending on your level of conditioning, sparring rounds can range anywhere from one to five minutes. Each round is separated by either 30-second, one-minute or two-minute breaks. A good sparring session consists of at least five to eight rounds.

Since sparring workouts are structured around time, you will need a good workout timer. Most workout timers will allow you to adjust your round lengths anywhere from 30 seconds to 9 minutes. Rest periods can be changed from 30 seconds to 5 minutes depending on your level of conditioning and training goals.

When You Get Hit!

If and when you get hit in a sparring session, stay in control of your emotions and don't panic. Keep both hands up, stay mobile, and remain defensively alert. Maintain proper breathing, employ positive self-talk, and don't allow negative thoughts to contaminate your mind. Stay focused on the task at hand and continue to look for openings in your training partner's defenses.

Here are ten common mistakes that are made when sparring. Overcoming these errors will significantly enhance your killer instinct.

1. Quitting or giving up after being hit.

2. Being distracted (internally or externally) when fighting.

3. Fearful or excessive blinking.

4. Randomly throwing punches or failing to focus on a particular target.

5. Lack of commitment when attacking your partner.

6. Hesitating or over thinking.

7. Turning your head away or closing your eyes when a blow is thrown at you.

8. Turning your body completely sideways from the sparring partner.

9. Running away from your opponent's attack.

10. Nervously swatting your sparring partner's boxing glove.

8. Hip Fusing Drill

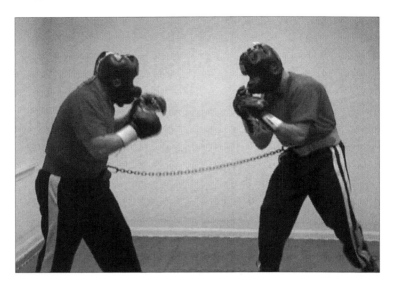

If you want an exercise that will help you build courage, look no further than hip fusing. Hip fusing is an advanced form of full-contact sparring that requires tethering yourself to your partner with a heavy-duty chain. To perform the hip fusing drill, place a weight lifting belt on each participant.

Next, attach a heavy-duty chain (approximately 4 feet in length) to each belt. The length of the chain will depend on your skill level. For example, a longer chain would be used for beginners who need more defensive reaction time to defend against the blows.

A word of caution: Prematurely engaging in hip fusing drills can be dangerous and counterproductive. Remember, hip fusing is for advanced practitioners who have a solid foundation in full-contact sparring. Never participate in hip fusing until you have acquired the following skills:

- A strong foundation in both offense and defensive skills.

- The ability to control the force of your offensive techniques.

- The fundamental attributes of unarmed combat (i.e. speed, timing, coordination, accuracy, balance, and the ability not to telegraph your movements.

- A safe attitude toward training.

9. The Gauntlet Drill

The gauntlet drill builds is another great drill for developing characteristics of the killer instinct. To perform this exercise, you will need a minimum of ten people, each one holding a focus mitt. Divide the ten people into two equal rows and make certain they hold the glove at approximately head level.

Next, have the designated striker start from the top of the rows. From a fighting stance, have him deliver a lead straight/rear cross combination in a crisscross fashion while steadily moving down the two rows. Once he works his way through the "gauntlet," he should quickly return to the starting position (top of the row) and begins again. A good workout would be to perform this drill for 10 minutes non-stop.

10. Heavy Bag Training

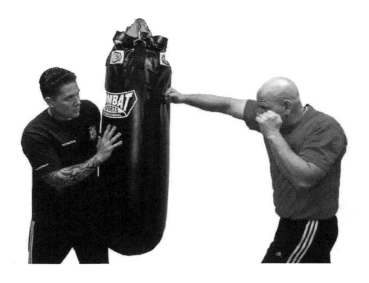

Heavy bag training also builds instrumental aggression of the killer instinct and it's a staple training exercise for boxing, kick boxing, mixed martial arts, and self-defense. It's also popular among people who just want to stay in shape or add a new dimension to their fitness programs. Many people use the heavy bag for some of the following reasons:

- It conditions the entire body.

- It improves muscular endurance.

- It strengthens bones, tendons, and ligaments.

- It conditions the cardiovascular system.

- It relieves stress and helps channel aggressive energy.

The heavy bag is constructed of either top grain leather, canvas or vinyl. Most bags are 14 inches in diameter and 42 inches in length. The interior of the bag is filled with either cotton fiber, thick foam, sand or other durable material. Depending on the brand, heavy bags can weigh anywhere from seventy-five to two hundred and fifty pounds. However, for our purposes, I suggest a bag that weighs a minimum of 150 pounds.

Safe and effective heavy bag training will require you to find a place that will allow both you and the bag to move around freely. The location should also be a relatively quiet place that is free of distractions. Here are a few places you might want to consider:

- Garage
- Carport
- Basement
- Barn
- Home gym
- Open field or backyard
- Warehouse
- Under a deck

Before you begin working out, invest in a good pair of bag gloves that will protect your hands when working out. When buying gloves, spare no expense and look for a reputable and high-quality brand. This will provide years of reliable use and will help ensure a better quality workout.

If you don't think you'll need bag gloves, think again. Striking the heavy bag without hand protection causes sore knuckles, bruised bones, hand inflammation, sore wrists and scraped knuckles. As a result, it will set your training back for several weeks in order for your hands to heal.

A good heavy bag workout consists of at least five rounds lasting three minutes in duration. However, there are other heavy bag drills that you can add to your routine, like the Elevation Drill.

The Elevation Drill

The elevation drill develops fighting skills while building several elements of the killer instinct including instrumental aggression. The objective of this exercise is to keep the heavy bag elevated at a 45-degree angle by continuously punching it. This drill is brutal on the arms. In fact, the average person can barely last 30 seconds. To perform the exercise follow these steps:

1. Face the heavy bag and assume a fighting stance.

2. Deliver the lead straight and rear cross combination continuously. Concentrate on delivering full-speed, full-force punches.

3. Maintain a rapid-fire cadence to keep the bag elevated at a 45-degree angle from the floor.

4. Avoid pushing the bag, remember to snap each blow.

5. Perform the drill for a total of 5 rounds. Each round should last anywhere from 30 to 60 seconds. If you are exceptionally conditioned, go for 90 seconds.

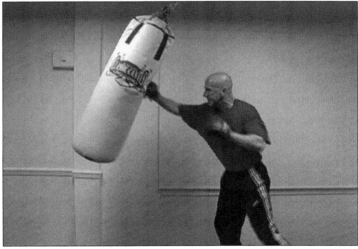

Here, a student performs the elevation drill.

The Pummel Drill

The pummel drill is another great drill. Pummeling requires you to attack a heavy bag or body opponent bag with a flurry of strikes from the top mounted position for specified period of time. To execute the pummel drill, apply the following steps:

1. Place a heavy bag on the floor.

2. Have your training partner tie a rope (approximately five feet long) to the top of the bag.

3. Mount the heavy bag (the same way you would mount an assailant in a ground fight).

4. For 30 seconds employ full-speed, full-force strikes on the upper portion of the heavy bag. Be vicious and attack the back with all of the aggression you can muster. There are two punches that can be delivered effectively from this position: linear punches and hammer fist strikes.

5. Have your training partner pull vigorously (side to side, and up and down) on the rope while you deliver the blows. Strive to maintain a good base and avoid losing your balance when

your partner tugs the bag.

6. Rest for one minute, and then repeat the process for a total of ten sets.

Here are some important tips when working out on the bag:

- Always warm up with some light stretching and calisthenics before working out.

- Gradually build up the force of your blows. Remember, a beginner's wrists are too weak to accommodate full-force punches.

- Never sacrifice balance for power.

- Remember to snap your punches.

- Always keep your wrists straight when striking the bag.

- Always maintain proper form.

- Move around and avoid remaining stationary.

- Learn to integrate your kicks, punches, and strikes into logical compound attacks.

- Pace yourself to avoid premature exhaustion.

- Don't wear jewelry or a watch when training.

- Stay relaxed and avoid unnecessary muscular tension.

- Never hold your breath. Remember to exhale with the delivery of each and every technique.

- Avoid the urge to stop the bag from moving. Let it swing freely!

- If you don't know the proper way to throw a punch or kick, get instruction from a qualified coach or instructor.

- Avoid heavy bag training two days in a row. Give your body a few days to recover from your last workout.

Chapter Three
Killer Instinct Workout Programs

The 10 Best Ways to Develop Your Killer Instinct

Creating a Killer Instinct Program

We are now going to take all of the knowledge from the previous chapters and put it into a training program. In this section, I'm going to show you how to design a solid killer instinct training program to suit your personal needs. However, before we begin, you must be certain that your program meets the following criteria.

- **Realistic** - your training should be as real as possible. It should include drills and exercises that replicate real world scenarios and conditions.

- **Simple** - your training should be easy to put into action. It should not require time-consuming preparation or expensive or complex equipment.

- **Specific** - your training should meet specific training goals. This might be a micro goal, such as improving your instrumental aggression during a particular training drill.

The 10 Best Ways to Develop Your Killer Instinct

- **Stressful** - your training should produce one or more of the six types of stressors (i.e., acute emotional stress, mental confusion, mental fatigue, physical fatigue (muscular or aerobic), physical discomfort or pain, and environmental stress).

- **Quantifiable** - you must be able to accurately measure your progress in training. Performance measurement is motivational and helps you stay committed to your goals. It also useful for identifying methodologies that are not helping you reach your personal objectives.

Sample Killer Instinct Programs

Let me start by saying, there's no single program that works for everyone. Since each of us has different goals, and time-lines, it's up to you to identify your needs and personalize your training accordingly. The bottom line is, only you can determine what works best for you.

There are many ways to set up a killer instinct program. In fact, some of you might want to first consult with your coach, trainer or instructor prior to setting up a program and schedule.

How to do it...

What follows is a sample program utilizing both physical and cognitive killer instinct exercises. Once again, these just serve as examples of what you can do.

STEP 1: IDENTIFY YOUR GOAL: For this example, our immediate goal is to develop and improve instrumental aggression of the killer instinct.

STEP 2: SELECT YOUR DRILLS: Choose from the list of killer instinct drills (both mental and physical) that develop this particular attribute. In this case, you will choose from the list below:

Physical Drills:

- Impact training
- Medicine ball
- Hip fusing
- Gauntlet drill
- Sparring
- Heavy Bag Training

Mental Drills:

- Visualization
- Meditation
- Controlled breathing
- Bifurcation drills

STEP 3: DETERMINE YOUR TRAINING FREQUENCY: Now, decide how many days per week your schedule permits you to train.

Example 1: Training 5 days per week

In this example, you will actively train five days per week.

MONDAY: • Meditation • Sparring
TUESDAY: • Visualization session • Controlled breathing exercises
WEDNESDAY: (rest day)
THURSDAY: • Visualization session • Controlled breathing exercises • Hip fusing
FRIDAY: • Bifurcation training • Heavy bag training • Meditation
SATURDAY: (rest day)
SUNDAY: • Meditation • Gauntlet drill

Example 2: Training 3 days per week

This weekly program is a bit more conservative, it requires you to train three days per week.

MONDAY: • Sparring • Visualization • Controlled breathing exercises
TUESDAY: (rest day)
WEDNESDAY: • Impact training • Meditation • Controlled breathing exercises
THURSDAY: (rest day)
FRIDAY: • Bifurcation training • Hip fusing • Medicine ball training • Meditation
SATURDAY: (rest day)   **SUNDAY:** (rest day)

Example 3: Training cognitive exercises only

This program requires you to practice cognitive exercises exclusively. This form of training is helpful for individuals who are unable to physically workout because of a training injury.

MONDAY:

- Controlled breathing exercises
- Visualization

TUESDAY:

- (rest day)

WEDNESDAY:

- Controlled breathing exercises
- Meditation

THURSDAY:

- Consultation with coach, instructor or mentor
- Meditation
- Controlled breathing exercises

FRIDAY:

- Visualization

SATURDAY: (rest day)

SUNDAY: (rest day)

Killer Instinct Program Tips

- Devote a least one month to the program before changing things around.

- Try to get at least two visualization and meditation sessions per week. If you can do more, even better.

- Visualization techniques can be performed before, during or after physical training.

- Meditation sessions can be conducted before or after physical training.

- Controlled breathing exercises can be conducted before, during or after physical training.

- After one month, feel free to change things around. Remember, nothing is set in stone.

- Encourage friendly and healthy competition between your training partner.

- Always maintain a professional attitude when training.

- Don't expect to be perfect when training.

- Don't let incorrect habits go uncorrected.

- Don't get frustrated. Remember, it's a learning process that takes time.

- Make full use of your rest days. Remember, resting the body is just as important as training. Training intensely day after day will lead to either burnout or injury. The body needs time to recoup and replenish itself from grueling workouts. Remember, there is growth in rest.

- Since physical fitness goals will vary from person to person, you'll need to incorporate your current fitness/workout regimen (i.e., weight training, CrossFit, cardio training, etc.) into your program. How you do this, is entirely up to you.

Finding the Right Training Partner

As I discussed earlier, some of these killer instinct exercises can be performed individually, while others will require the assistance of a training partner, instructor or coach.

A good training partner should motivate, challenge and push you to your limits. He or she doesn't have to share the same goals as you do, but they must be willing to help you reach your full potential. Your training partner or coach should also be somewhat familiar with the various combat drills and equipment. For example, they should know how to hold and manipulate the focus mitts, perform training simulations, and perform full-contact exercises.

While a good training partner can be a major asset, having a bad one can be a major liability. Be exceptionally careful who you choose to train with you. When looking for a training parter, try to avoid the following personality types:

1. **The conversationalist** - someone who talks too much and often disrupts the training intensity.

2. **The challenger** - someone who is naturally argumentative and tries to test your knowledge and patience.

3. **The ego tripper** - someone who will do anything to prove just how tough he is. He usually enjoys full-contact drills and likes to injure others in training.

4. **The insecure one** - someone who is hesitant to participate in training full-contact drills and exercises.

5. **The know-it-all** - someone who thinks he knows anything and everything about mental toughness training.

6. **The dilettante** - someone who doesn't understand the importance of mental toughness training, and therefore doesn't fully commit himself to the program.

Finally, remember that a good training partner or coach is there to evaluate your performance during your workouts. Listen carefully to what he has to say. A good coach, for example, will be brutally honest and tell you what you are doing correctly and what you are doing wrong. Learn to put your ego aside and heed his advice.

Safety When Training

Safety precautions must always be taken when engaged in training. Remember, a serious injury can set you back for weeks and even months. Don't make the mistake of letting your ego or laziness get the best of you. Learn to be safety-conscious. Here are a few suggestions to help minimize the possibilities of injury when training:

1. Buy the best training equipment that you can afford.

2. Know the proper way to use training equipment.

3. Regularly inspect your equipment for wear and defects.

4. Avoid ego-driven training partners or coaches.

5. Be especially aware when training with someone of superior size, skill, or experience.

6. Always warm up before training.

7. Drink plenty of water during training sessions to avoid dehydration.

8. Be cautious when performing training drills for the first time.

It's also a good idea to have a first-aid kit nearby. A first-aid kit is intended for both minor and major injuries. The kit should be kept in a well-sealed box away from children. Don't forget to write down the emergency number for your local hospital or medical clinic on the box. Most first-aid kits can be purchased at your local drugstore. Each kit should contain cotton wool and hydrogen peroxide for cleaning cuts, tweezers, scissors, triangular bandages, alcohol swabs, adhesive tape, adhesive bandages, antibiotic ointment, sterile pads, gauze bandages, and elastic bandages for sprains and for elbow and knee injuries.

Avoiding Overtraining & Burnout

Burnout is defined as a negative emotional state acquired by physical overtraining. Some symptoms of burnout include physical illness, boredom, anxiety, disinterest in training, and general sluggish behavior. Whether you are a beginner or expert, you're susceptible to burnout. Here are a few suggestions to help avoid burnout in your training:

1. Make your workouts intense but enjoyable.
2. Vary your training routine (i.e., hard day/easy day routine).
3. Train to different types of music.
4. Pace yourself during your workouts - don't try to do it all in one day.
5. Listen to your body- if you don't feel up to training, skip a day.
6. Work out in different types of environments.
7. Use different types of training equipment.
8. Workout with different training partners.
9. Keep accurate records of your training routine.

10. Vary the intensity of your training throughout your workout.

Keeping Track of Your Training

In order to reap the full benefits of training, you need to keep track of your workouts and monitor your progress. Monitoring your training will give you a wide range of benefits, including:

1. Help determine if you making progress in your training.

2. The ability to effectively alter your training program.

3. Track your rate of progress,

4. Stay interested and motivated.

5. Break through performance plateaus.

Two of the best tools for keeping track of your training progress are: the training journal and video footage. Let's take a look at each one.

The Training Journal

Record keeping is one of the most important and often neglected aspects of training. Try to make it a habit to keep accurate records of your workouts in a personal journal. This type of record keeping is important for some of the following reasons:

1. It will help you monitor your progress.

2. It will keep you organized.

3. It will inspire, motivate and remind you to stick to your goals.

4. It helps prevent potential injuries.

The 10 Best Ways to Develop Your Killer Instinct

5. It will help you guard against over training.

6. If you are learning new skills, it accelerates the learning process.

7. It gives you valuable training information that can be analyzed.

8. It helps you determine which drills, activities, and exercises are unproductive.

9. It helps you determine which activities are helpful and productive.

10. When making entries into your journal, don't forget to include some of the following important details:

11. The date and time you trained.

12. The killer instinct skill or attribute you are training.

13. The types of drills and exercises you performed.

14. The number or sets, reps you performed for each exercise or drill.

15. The number or rounds and minutes per round you performed for each drill or exercise.

16. The feelings you experienced before, during, and after your workout.

17. Your overall mood.

18. Concerns you have about your current training.

19. Comments, ideas and observations made by your coach, training partner or instructor.

Videotaping

If you really want to actually see your progress, videotape your workouts. The video will provide you with a more accurate picture of what you are doing in your training. You will be able to observe mistakes and recognize your strengths and weaknesses. The video footage will also motivate you to train harder. Remember to date each videotape or video clip; later on you will be able to compare and see marked improvements in your training performance.

The 10 Best Ways to Develop Your Killer Instinct

Glossary

The following terms are defined in the context of Contemporary Fighting Arts and its related concepts. In many instances, the definitions bear little resemblance to those found in a standard dictionary.

A

accuracy—The precise or exact projection of force. Accuracy is also defined as the ability to execute a combative movement with precision and exactness.

adaptability—The ability to physically and psychologically adjust to new or different conditions or circumstances of combat.

advanced first-strike tools—Offensive techniques that are specifically used when confronted with multiple opponents.

aerobic exercise—Literally, "with air." Exercise that elevates the heart rate to a training level for a prolonged period of time, usually 30 minutes.

affective preparedness – One of the three components of preparedness. Affective preparedness means being emotionally, philosophically, and spiritually prepared for the strains of combat. See cognitive preparedness and psychomotor preparedness.

aggression—Hostile and injurious behavior directed toward a person.

aggressive response—One of the three possible counters when assaulted by a grab, choke, or hold from a standing position. Aggressive response requires you to counter the enemy with destructive blows and strikes. See moderate response and passive response.

aggressive hand positioning—Placement of hands so as to imply aggressive or hostile intentions.

agility—An attribute of combat. One's ability to move his or her body quickly and gracefully.

amalgamation—A scientific process of uniting or merging.

ambidextrous—The ability to perform with equal facility on both the right and left sides of the body.

anabolic steroids – synthetic chemical compounds that resemble the male sex hormone testosterone. This performance-enhancing drug is known to increase lean muscle mass, strength, and endurance.

analysis and integration—One of the five elements of CFA's mental component. This is the painstaking process of breaking down various elements, concepts, sciences, and disciplines into their atomic parts, and then methodically and strategically analyzing, experimenting, and drastically modifying the information so that it fulfills three combative requirements: efficiency, effectiveness, and safety. Only then is it finally integrated into the CFA system.

anatomical striking targets—The various anatomical body targets that can be struck and which are especially vulnerable to potential harm. They include: the eyes, temple, nose, chin, back of neck, front of neck, solar plexus, ribs, groin, thighs, knees, shins, and instep.

anchoring – The strategic process of trapping the assailant's neck or limb in order to control the range of engagement during razing.

assailant—A person who threatens or attacks another person.

assault—The threat or willful attempt to inflict injury upon the person of another.

assault and battery—The unlawful touching of another person without justification.

assessment—The process of rapidly gathering, analyzing, and accurately evaluating information in terms of threat and danger. You can assess people, places, actions, and objects.

attack—Offensive action designed to physically control, injure, or kill another person.

attack by combination (ABC) - One of the five methods of attack. See compound attack.

attack by drawing (ABD) - One of the five methods of attack. A method of attack predicated on counterattack.

attitude—One of the three factors that determine who wins a street fight. Attitude means being emotionally, philosophically, and spiritually liberated from societal and religious mores. See skills and knowledge.

attributes of combat—The physical, mental, and spiritual qualities that enhance combat skills and tactics.

awareness—Perception or knowledge of people, places, actions, and objects. (In CFA, there are three categories of tactical awareness: criminal awareness, situational awareness, and self-awareness.)

B

balance—One's ability to maintain equilibrium while stationary or moving.

blading the body—Strategically positioning your body at a 45-degree angle.

blitz and disengage—A style of sparring whereby a fighter moves into a range of combat, unleashes a strategic compound attack, and then quickly disengages to a safe distance. Of all sparring methodologies, the blitz and disengage most closely resembles a real street fight.

block—A defensive tool designed to intercept the assailant's attack by placing a non-vital target between the assailant's strike and your vital body target.

body composition—The ratio of fat to lean body tissue.

body language—Nonverbal communication through posture, gestures, and facial expressions.

body mechanics—Technically precise body movement during the execution of a body weapon, defensive technique, or other fighting maneuver.

body tackle – A tackle that occurs when your opponent haphazardly rushes forward and plows his body into yours.

body weapon—Also known as a tool, one of the various body parts that can be used to strike or otherwise injure or kill a criminal assailant.

burn out—A negative emotional state acquired by physically over- training. Some symptoms include: illness, boredom, anxiety, disinterest in training, and general sluggishness.

C

cadence—Coordinating tempo and rhythm to establish a timing pattern of movement.

cardiorespiratory conditioning—The component of physical fitness that deals with the heart, lungs, and circulatory system.

centerline—An imaginary vertical line that divides your body in half and which contains many of your vital anatomical targets.

choke holds—Holds that impair the flow of blood or oxygen to the brain.

circular movements—Movements that follow the direction of a curve.

close-quarter combat—One of the three ranges of knife and

bludgeon combat. At this distance, you can strike, slash, or stab your assailant with a variety of close-quarter techniques.

cognitive development—One of the five elements of CFA's mental component. The process of developing and enhancing your fighting skills through specific mental exercises and techniques. See analysis and integration, killer instinct, philosophy, and strategic/tactical development.

cognitive exercises—Various mental exercises used to enhance fighting skills and tactics.

cognitive preparedness – One of the three components of preparedness. Cognitive preparedness means being equipped with the strategic concepts, principles, and general knowledge of combat. See affective preparedness and psychomotor preparedness.

combat-oriented training—Training that is specifically related to the harsh realities of both armed and unarmed combat. See ritual-oriented training and sport-oriented training.

combative arts—The various arts of war. See martial arts.

combative attributes—See attributes of combat.

combative fitness—A state characterized by cardiorespiratory and muscular/skeletal conditioning, as well as proper body composition.

combative mentality—Also known as the killer instinct, this is a combative state of mind necessary for fighting. See killer instinct.

combat ranges—The various ranges of unarmed combat.

combative utility—The quality of condition of being combatively useful.

combination(s)—See compound attack.

common peroneal nerve—A pressure point area located approximately four to six inches above the knee on the midline of the outside of the thigh.

composure—A combative attribute. Composure is a quiet and focused mind-set that enables you to acquire your combative agenda.

compound attack—One of the five conventional methods of attack. Two or more body weapons launched in strategic succession whereby the fighter overwhelms his assailant with a flurry of full speed, full-force blows.

conditioning training—A CFA training methodology requiring the practitioner to deliver a variety of offensive and defensive combinations for a 4-minute period. See proficiency training and street training.

contact evasion—Physically moving or manipulating your body to avoid being tackled by the adversary.

Contemporary Fighting Arts—A modern martial art and self-defense system made up of three parts: physical, mental, and spiritual.

conventional ground-fighting tools—Specific ground-fighting techniques designed to control, restrain, and temporarily incapacitate your adversary. Some conventional ground fighting tactics include: submission holds, locks, certain choking techniques, and specific striking techniques.

coordination—A physical attribute characterized by the ability to perform a technique or movement with efficiency, balance, and accuracy.

counterattack—Offensive action made to counter an assailant's initial attack.

courage—A combative attribute. The state of mind and spirit that enables a fighter to face danger and vicissitudes with confidence, resolution, and bravery.

creatine monohydrate—A tasteless and odorless white powder that mimics some of the effects of anabolic steroids. Creatine is a safe body-building product that can benefit anyone who wants to increase their strength, endurance, and lean muscle mass.

criminal awareness—One of the three categories of CFA awareness. It involves a general understanding and knowledge of the nature and dynamics of a criminal's motivations, mentalities, methods, and capabilities to perpetrate violent crime. See situational awareness and self-awareness.

criminal justice—The study of criminal law and the procedures associated with its enforcement.

criminology—The scientific study of crime and criminals.

cross-stepping—The process of crossing one foot in front of or behind the other when moving.

crushing tactics—Nuclear grappling-range techniques designed to crush the assailant's anatomical targets.

D

deadly force—Weapons or techniques that may result in unconsciousness, permanent disfigurement, or death.

deception—A combative attribute. A stratagem whereby you delude your assailant.

decisiveness—A combative attribute. The ability to follow a tactical course of action that is unwavering and focused.

defense—The ability to strategically thwart an assailant's attack (armed or unarmed).

defensive flow—A progression of continuous defensive responses.

defensive mentality—A defensive mind-set.

defensive reaction time—The elapsed time between an assailant's physical attack and your defensive response to that attack. See offensive reaction time.

demeanor—A person's outward behavior. One of the essential factors to consider when assessing a threatening individual.

diet—A lifestyle of healthy eating.

disingenuous vocalization—The strategic and deceptive utilization of words to successfully launch a preemptive strike at your adversary.

distancing—The ability to quickly understand spatial relationships and how they relate to combat.

distractionary tactics—Various verbal and physical tactics designed to distract your adversary.

double-end bag—A small leather ball hung from the ceiling and anchored to the floor with bungee cord. It helps develop striking accuracy, speed, timing, eye-hand coordination, footwork and overall defensive skills.

double-leg takedown—A takedown that occurs when your opponent shoots for both of your legs to force you to the ground.

E

ectomorph—One of the three somatotypes. A body type characterized by a high degree of slenderness, angularity, and fragility. See endomorph and mesomorph.

effectiveness—One of the three criteria for a CFA body weapon, technique, tactic, or maneuver. It means the ability to produce a desired effect. See efficiency and safety.

efficiency—One of the three criteria for a CFA body weapon, technique, tactic, or maneuver. It means the ability to reach an objective quickly and economically. See effectiveness and safety.

emotionless—A combative attribute. Being temporarily devoid of human feeling.

endomorph—One of the three somatotypes. A body type characterized by a high degree of roundness, softness, and body fat. See ectomorph and mesomorph.

evasion—A defensive maneuver that allows you to strategically maneuver your body away from the assailant's strike.

evasive sidestepping—Evasive footwork where the practitioner moves to either the right or left side.

evasiveness—A combative attribute. The ability to avoid threat or danger.

excessive force—An amount of force that exceeds the need for a particular event and is unjustified in the eyes of the law.

experimentation—The painstaking process of testing a combative hypothesis or theory.

explosiveness—A combative attribute that is characterized by a sudden outburst of violent energy.

F

fear—A strong and unpleasant emotion caused by the anticipation or awareness of threat or danger. There are three stages of fear in order of intensity: fright, panic, and terror. See fright, panic, and terror.

feeder—A skilled technician who manipulates the focus mitts.

femoral nerve—A pressure point area located approximately 6 inches above the knee on the inside of the thigh.

fighting stance—Any one of the stances used in CFA's system. A strategic posture you can assume when face-to-face with an unarmed assailant(s). The fighting stance is generally used after you have launched your first-strike tool.

fight-or-flight syndrome—A response of the sympathetic nervous system to a fearful and threatening situation, during which it prepares your body to either fight or flee from the perceived danger.

finesse—A combative attribute. The ability to skillfully execute a movement or a series of movements with grace and refinement.

first strike—Proactive force used to interrupt the initial stages of an assault before it becomes a self-defense situation.

first-strike principle—A CFA principle that states that when physical danger is imminent and you have no other tactical option but to fight back, you should strike first, strike fast, and strike with authority and keep the pressure on.

first-strike stance—One of the stances used in CFA's system. A strategic posture used prior to initiating a first strike.

first-strike tools—Specific offensive tools designed to initiate a preemptive strike against your adversary.

fisted blows – Hand blows delivered with a clenched fist.

five tactical options – The five strategic responses you can make in a self-defense situation, listed in order of increasing level of resistance: comply, escape, de-escalate, assert, and fight back.

flexibility—The muscles' ability to move through maximum natural ranges. See muscular/skeletal conditioning.

focus mitts—Durable leather hand mitts used to develop and sharpen offensive and defensive skills.

footwork—Quick, economical steps performed on the balls of the feet while you are relaxed, alert, and balanced. Footwork is structured around four general movements: forward, backward, right, and left.

fractal tool—Offensive or defensive tools that can be used in more than one combat range.

fright—The first stage of fear; quick and sudden fear. See panic and terror.

full Beat – One of the four beat classifications in the Widow Maker Program. The full beat strike has a complete initiation and retraction phase.

G

going postal - a slang term referring to a person who suddenly and unexpectedly attacks you with an explosive and frenzied flurry of blows. Also known as postal attack.

grappling range—One of the three ranges of unarmed combat. Grappling range is the closest distance of unarmed combat from which you can employ a wide variety of close-quarter tools and techniques. The grappling range of unarmed combat is also divided into two planes: vertical (standing) and horizontal (ground fighting). See kicking range and punching range.

grappling-range tools—The various body tools and techniques that are employed in the grappling range of unarmed combat, including head butts; biting, tearing, clawing, crushing, and gouging tactics; foot stomps, horizontal, vertical, and diagonal elbow strikes, vertical and diagonal knee strikes, chokes, strangles, joint locks, and holds. See punching range tools and kicking range tools.

ground fighting—Also known as the horizontal grappling plane, this is fighting that takes place on the ground.

guard—Also known as the hand guard, this refers to a fighter's hand positioning.

guard position—Also known as leg guard or scissors hold, this is a ground-fighting position in which a fighter is on his back holding his opponent between his legs.

H

half beat – One of the four beat classifications in the Widow Maker Program. The half beat strike is delivered through the retraction phase of the proceeding strike.

hand immobilization attack (HIA) - One of the five methods of attack. A method of attack whereby the practitioner traps his opponent's limb or limbs in order to execute an offense attack of his own.

hand positioning—See guard.

hand wraps—Long strips of cotton that are wrapped around the hands and wrists for greater protection.

haymaker—A wild and telegraphed swing of the arms executed by an unskilled fighter.

head-hunter—A fighter who primarily attacks the head.

heavy bag—A large cylindrical bag used to develop kicking, punching, or striking power.

high-line kick—One of the two different classifications of a kick. A kick that is directed to targets above an assailant's waist level. See low-line kick.

hip fusing—A full-contact drill that teaches a fighter to "stand his ground" and overcome the fear of exchanging blows with a stronger opponent. This exercise is performed by connecting two fighters with a 3-foot chain, forcing them to fight in the punching range of unarmed combat.

histrionics—The field of theatrics or acting.

hook kick—A circular kick that can be delivered in both kicking and punching ranges.

hook punch—A circular punch that can be delivered in both the punching and grappling ranges.

I

impact power—Destructive force generated by mass and velocity.

impact training—A training exercise that develops pain tolerance.

incapacitate—To disable an assailant by rendering him unconscious or damaging his bones, joints, or organs.

initiative—Making the first offensive move in combat.

inside position—The area between the opponent's arms, where he has the greatest amount of control.

intent—One of the essential factors to consider when assessing a threatening individual. The assailant's purpose or motive. See demeanor, positioning, range, and weapon capability.

intuition—The innate ability to know or sense something without the use of rational thought.

J

jeet kune do (JKD) - "Way of the intercepting fist." Bruce Lee's approach to the martial arts, which includes his innovative concepts, theories, methodologies, and philosophies.

jersey Pull – Strategically pulling the assailant's shirt or jacket over his head as he disengages from the clinch position.

joint lock—A grappling-range technique that immobilizes the assailant's joint.

K

kick—A sudden, forceful strike with the foot.

kicking range—One of the three ranges of unarmed combat. Kicking range is the furthest distance of unarmed combat wherein you use your legs to strike an assailant. See grappling range and punching range.

kicking-range tools—The various body weapons employed in the kicking range of unarmed combat, including side kicks, push kicks, hook kicks, and vertical kicks.

killer instinct—A cold, primal mentality that surges to your consciousness and turns you into a vicious fighter.

kinesics—The study of nonlinguistic body movement communications. (For example, eye movement, shrugs, or facial gestures.)

kinesiology—The study of principles and mechanics of human movement.

kinesthetic perception—The ability to accurately feel your body during the execution of a particular movement.

knowledge—One of the three factors that determine who will win a street fight. Knowledge means knowing and understanding how to fight. See skills and attitude.

L

lead side -The side of the body that faces an assailant.

leg guard—See guard position.

linear movement—Movements that follow the path of a straight line.

low-maintenance tool—Offensive and defensive tools that require the least amount of training and practice to maintain proficiency. Low maintenance tools generally do not require preliminary stretching.

low-line kick—One of the two different classifications of a kick. A kick that is directed to targets below the assailant's waist level. (See high-line kick.)

lock—See joint lock.

M

maneuver—To manipulate into a strategically desired position.

MAP—An acronym that stands for moderate, aggressive, passive. MAP provides the practitioner with three possible responses to various grabs, chokes, and holds that occur from a standing position. See aggressive response, moderate response, and passive response.

martial arts—The "arts of war."

masking—The process of concealing your true feelings from your opponent by manipulating and managing your body language.

mechanics—(See body mechanics.)

mental attributes—The various cognitive qualities that enhance your fighting skills.

mental component—One of the three vital components of the CFA system. The mental component includes the cerebral aspects of fighting including the killer instinct, strategic and tactical development, analysis and integration, philosophy, and cognitive development. See physical component and spiritual component.

mesomorph—One of the three somatotypes. A body type classified by a high degree of muscularity and strength. The mesomorph possesses the ideal physique for unarmed combat. See ectomorph and endomorph.

mobility—A combative attribute. The ability to move your body quickly and freely while balanced. See footwork.

moderate response—One of the three possible counters when assaulted by a grab, choke, or hold from a standing position. Moderate response requires you to counter your opponent with a control and restraint (submission hold). See aggressive response and passive response.

modern martial art—A pragmatic combat art that has evolved to meet the demands and characteristics of the present time.

mounted position—A dominant ground-fighting position where a fighter straddles his opponent.

muscular endurance—The muscles' ability to perform the same motion or task repeatedly for a prolonged period of time.

muscular flexibility—The muscles' ability to move through maximum natural ranges.

muscular strength—The maximum force that can be exerted by a particular muscle or muscle group against resistance.

muscular/skeletal conditioning—An element of physical fitness that entails muscular strength, endurance, and flexibility.

N

naked choke—A throat choke executed from the chest to back position. This secure choke is executed with two hands and it can be performed while standing, kneeling, and ground fighting with the opponent.

neck crush – A powerful pain compliance technique used when the adversary buries his head in your chest to avoid being razed.

neutralize—See incapacitate.

neutral zone—The distance outside the kicking range at which neither the practitioner nor the assailant can touch the other.

nonaggressive physiology—Strategic body language used prior to initiating a first strike.

nontelegraphic movement—Body mechanics or movements that do not inform an assailant of your intentions.

nuclear ground-fighting tools—Specific grappling range tools designed to inflict immediate and irreversible damage. Nuclear tools and tactics include biting tactics, tearing tactics, crushing tactics, continuous choking tactics, gouging techniques, raking tactics, and all striking techniques.

O

offense—The armed and unarmed means and methods of attacking a criminal assailant.

offensive flow—Continuous offensive movements (kicks, blows, and strikes) with unbroken continuity that ultimately neutralize or terminate the opponent. See compound attack.

offensive reaction time—The elapsed time between target selection and target impaction.

one-mindedness—A state of deep concentration wherein you are free from all distractions (internal and external).

ostrich defense—One of the biggest mistakes one can make when defending against an opponent. This is when the practitioner looks away from that which he fears (punches, kicks, and strikes). His mentality is, "If I can't see it, it can't hurt me."

P

pain tolerance—Your ability to physically and psychologically withstand pain.

panic—The second stage of fear; overpowering fear. See fright and terror.

parry—A defensive technique: a quick, forceful slap that redirects an assailant's linear attack. There are two types of parries: horizontal and vertical.

passive response—One of the three possible counters when assaulted by a grab, choke, or hold from a standing position. Passive response requires you to nullify the assault without injuring your adversary. See aggressive response and moderate response.

patience—A combative attribute. The ability to endure and tolerate difficulty.

perception—Interpretation of vital information acquired from your senses when faced with a potentially threatening situation.

philosophical resolution—The act of analyzing and answering various questions concerning the use of violence in defense of yourself and others.

philosophy—One of the five aspects of CFA's mental component. A deep state of introspection whereby you methodically resolve critical questions concerning the use of force in defense of yourself or others.

physical attributes—The numerous physical qualities that enhance your combative skills and abilities.

physical component—One of the three vital components of the CFA system. The physical component includes the physical aspects of fighting, such as physical fitness, weapon/technique mastery, and combative attributes. See mental component and spiritual component.

physical conditioning—See combative fitness.

physical fitness—See combative fitness.

positional asphyxia—The arrangement, placement, or positioning of your opponent's body in such a way as to interrupt your breathing and cause unconsciousness or possibly death.

positioning—The spatial relationship of the assailant to the assailed person in terms of target exposure, escape, angle of attack, and various other strategic considerations.

postal attack - see going postal.

power—A physical attribute of armed and unarmed combat. The amount of force you can generate when striking an anatomical target.

power generators—Specific points on your body that generate impact power. There are three anatomical power generators: shoulders, hips, and feet.

precision—See accuracy.

preemptive strike—See first strike.

premise—An axiom, concept, rule, or any other valid reason to modify or go beyond that which has been established.

preparedness—A state of being ready for combat. There are three components of preparedness: affective preparedness, cognitive preparedness, and psychomotor preparedness.

probable reaction dynamics - The opponent's anticipated or predicted movements or actions during both armed and unarmed combat.

proficiency training—A CFA training methodology requiring the practitioner to execute a specific body weapon, technique, maneuver, or tactic over and over for a prescribed number of repetitions. See conditioning training and street training.

progressive indirect attack (PIA) – One of the five methods of attack. A progressive method of attack whereby the initial tool or technique is designed to set the opponent up for follow-up blows.

proxemics—The study of the nature and effect of man's personal space.

proximity—The ability to maintain a strategically safe distance from a threatening individual.

pseudospeciation—A combative attribute. The tendency to assign subhuman and inferior qualities to a threatening assailant.

psychological conditioning—The process of conditioning the mind for the horrors and rigors of real combat.

psychomotor preparedness—One of the three components of preparedness. Psychomotor preparedness means possessing all of the physical skills and attributes necessary to defeat a formidable adversary. See affective preparedness and cognitive preparedness.

punch—A quick, forceful strike of the fists.

punching range—One of the three ranges of unarmed combat. Punching range is the mid range of unarmed combat from which the fighter uses his hands to strike his assailant. See kicking range and grappling range.

punching-range tools—The various body weapons that are employed in the punching range of unarmed combat, including finger jabs, palm-heel strikes, rear cross, knife-hand strikes, horizontal and shovel hooks, uppercuts, and hammer-fist strikes. See grappling-range tools and kicking-range tools.

Q

qualities of combat—See attributes of combat.

quarter beat - One of the four beat classifications of the Widow Maker Program. Quarter beat strikes never break contact with the assailant's face. Quarter beat strikes are primarily responsible for creating the psychological panic and trauma when Razing.

R

range—The spatial relationship between a fighter and a threatening assailant.

range deficiency—The inability to effectively fight and defend in all ranges of combat (armed and unarmed).

range manipulation—A combative attribute. The strategic manipulation of combat ranges.

range proficiency—A combative attribute. The ability to effectively fight and defend in all ranges of combat (armed and unarmed).

ranges of engagement—See combat ranges.

ranges of unarmed combat—The three distances (kicking range, punching range, and grappling range) a fighter might physically engage with an assailant while involved in unarmed combat.

raze – To level, demolish or obliterate.

razer – One who performs the Razing methodology.

razing – The second phase of the Widow Maker Program. A series of vicious close quarter techniques designed to physically and psychologically extirpate a criminal attacker.

razing amplifier - a technique, tactic or procedure that magnifies the destructiveness of your razing technique.

reaction dynamics—see probable reaction dynamics.

reaction time—The elapsed time between a stimulus and the response to that particular stimulus. See offensive reaction time and defensive reaction time.

rear cross—A straight punch delivered from the rear hand that crosses from right to left (if in a left stance) or left to right (if in a right stance).

rear side—The side of the body furthest from the assailant. See

The 10 Best Ways to Develop Your Killer Instinct

lead side.

reasonable force—That degree of force which is not excessive for a particular event and which is appropriate in protecting yourself or others.

refinement—The strategic and methodical process of improving or perfecting.

relocation principle—Also known as relocating, this is a street-fighting tactic that requires you to immediately move to a new location (usually by flanking your adversary) after delivering a compound attack.

repetition—Performing a single movement, exercise, strike, or action continuously for a specific period.

research—A scientific investigation or inquiry.

rhythm—Movements characterized by the natural ebb and flow of related elements.

ritual-oriented training—Formalized training that is conducted without intrinsic purpose. See combat-oriented training and sport-oriented training.

S

safety—One of the three criteria for a CFA body weapon, technique, maneuver, or tactic. It means that the tool, technique, maneuver or tactic provides the least amount of danger and risk for the practitioner. See efficiency and effectiveness.

scissors hold—See guard position.

scorching – Quickly and inconspicuously applying oleoresin capsicum (hot pepper extract) on your fingertips and then razing your adversary.

136

self-awareness—One of the three categories of CFA awareness. Knowing and understanding yourself. This includes aspects of yourself which may provoke criminal violence and which will promote a proper and strong reaction to an attack. See criminal awareness and situational awareness.

self-confidence—Having trust and faith in yourself.

self-enlightenment—The state of knowing your capabilities, limitations, character traits, feelings, general attributes, and motivations. See self-awareness.

set—A term used to describe a grouping of repetitions.

shadow fighting—A CFA training exercise used to develop and refine your tools, techniques, and attributes of armed and unarmed combat.

sharking – A counter attack technique that is used when your adversary grabs your razing hand.

shielding wedge - a defensive maneuver used to counter an unarmed postal attack.

simple direct attack (SDA) – One of the five methods of attack. A method of attack whereby the practitioner delivers a solitary offenses tool or technique. It may involve a series of discrete probes or one swift, powerful strike aimed at terminating the encounter.

situational awareness—One of the three categories of CFA awareness. A state of being totally alert to your immediate surroundings, including people, places, objects, and actions. (See criminal awareness and self-awareness.)

skeletal alignment—The proper alignment or arrangement of your body. Skeletal alignment maximizes the structural integrity of striking tools.

skills—One of the three factors that determine who will win a street fight. Skills refers to psychomotor proficiency with the tools and techniques of combat. See Attitude and Knowledge.

slipping—A defensive maneuver that permits you to avoid an assailant's linear blow without stepping out of range. Slipping can be accomplished by quickly snapping the head and upper torso sideways (right or left) to avoid the blow.

snap back—A defensive maneuver that permits you to avoid an assailant's linear and circular blows without stepping out of range. The snap back can be accomplished by quickly snapping the head backward to avoid the assailant's blow.

somatotypes—A method of classifying human body types or builds into three different categories: endomorph, mesomorph, and ectomorph. See endomorph, mesomorph, and ectomorph.

sparring—A training exercise where two or more fighters fight each other while wearing protective equipment.

speed—A physical attribute of armed and unarmed combat. The rate or a measure of the rapid rate of motion.

spiritual component—One of the three vital components of the CFA system. The spiritual component includes the metaphysical issues and aspects of existence. See physical component and mental component.

sport-oriented training—Training that is geared for competition and governed by a set of rules. See combat-oriented training and ritual-oriented training.

sprawling—A grappling technique used to counter a double- or single-leg takedown.

square off—To be face-to-face with a hostile or threatening assailant who is about to attack you.

stance—One of the many strategic postures you assume prior to or during armed or unarmed combat.

stick fighting—Fighting that takes place with either one or two sticks.

strategic positioning—Tactically positioning yourself to either escape, move behind a barrier, or use a makeshift weapon.

strategic/tactical development—One of the five elements of CFA's mental component.

strategy—A carefully planned method of achieving your goal of engaging an assailant under advantageous conditions.

street fight—A spontaneous and violent confrontation between two or more individuals wherein no rules apply.

street fighter—An unorthodox combatant who has no formal training. His combative skills and tactics are usually developed in the street by the process of trial and error.

street training—A CFA training methodology requiring the practitioner to deliver explosive compound attacks for 10 to 20 seconds. See condition ng training and proficiency training.

strength training—The process of developing muscular strength through systematic application of progressive resistance.

striking art—A combat art that relies predominantly on striking techniques to neutralize or terminate a criminal attacker.

striking shield—A rectangular shield constructed of foam and vinyl used to develop power in your kicks, punches, and strikes.

striking tool—A natural body weapon that impacts with the assailant's anatomical target.

strong side—The strongest and most coordinated side of your body.

structure—A definite and organized pattern.

style—The distinct manner in which a fighter executes or performs his combat skills.

stylistic integration—The purposeful and scientific collection of tools and techniques from various disciplines, which are strategically integrated and dramatically altered to meet three essential criteria: efficiency, effectiveness, and combative safety.

submission holds—Also known as control and restraint techniques, many of these locks and holds create sufficient pain to cause the adversary to submit.

system—The unification of principles, philosophies, rules, strategies, methodologies, tools, and techniques of a particular method of combat.

T

tactic—The skill of using the available means to achieve an end.

target awareness—A combative attribute that encompasses five strategic principles: target orientation, target recognition, target selection, target impaction, and target exploitation.

target exploitation—A combative attribute. The strategic maximization of your assailant's reaction dynamics during a fight. Target exploitation can be applied in both armed and unarmed encounters.

target impaction—The successful striking of the appropriate anatomical target.

target orientation—A combative attribute. Having a workable knowledge of the assailant's anatomical targets.

target recognition—The ability to immediately recognize appropriate anatomical targets during an emergency self-defense situation.

target selection—The process of mentally selecting the appropriate anatomical target for your self-defense situation. This is predicated on certain factors, including proper force response, assailant's positioning, and range.

target stare—A form of telegraphing in which you stare at the anatomical target you intend to strike.

target zones—The three areas in which an assailant's anatomical targets are located. (See zone one, zone two and zone three.)

technique—A systematic procedure by which a task is accomplished.

telegraphic cognizance—A combative attribute. The ability to recognize both verbal and non-verbal signs of aggression or assault.

telegraphing—Unintentionally making your intentions known to your adversary.

tempo—The speed or rate at which you speak.

terminate—To kill.

terror—The third stage of fear; defined as overpowering fear. See fright and panic.

timing—A physical and mental attribute of armed and unarmed combat. Your ability to execute a movement at the optimum moment.

tone—The overall quality or character of your voice.

tool—See body weapon.

traditional martial arts—Any martial art that fails to evolve and change to meet the demands and characteristics of its present environment.

traditional style/system—See traditional martial arts.

training drills—The various exercises and drills aimed at perfecting combat skills, attributes, and tactics.

trap and tuck – A counter move technique used when the adversary attempts to raze you during your quarter beat assault.

U

unified mind—A mind free and clear of distractions and focused on the combative situation.

use of force response—A combative attribute. Selecting the appropriate level of force for a particular emergency self-defense situation.

V

viciousness—A combative attribute. The propensity to be extremely violent and destructive often characterized by intense savagery.

violence—The intentional utilization of physical force to coerce, injure, cripple, or kill.

visualization—Also known as mental visualization or mental imagery. The purposeful formation of mental images and scenarios in the mind's eye.

W

warm-up—A series of mild exercises, stretches, and movements designed to prepare you for more intense exercise.

weak side—The weaker and more uncoordinated side of your body.

weapon and technique mastery—A component of CFA's physical component. The kinesthetic and psychomotor development of a weapon or combative technique.

weapon capability—An assailant's ability to use and attack with a particular weapon.

webbing - The first phase of the Widow Maker Program. Webbing is a two hand strike delivered to the assailant's chin. It is called Webbing because your hands resemble a large web that wraps around the enemy's face.

widow maker – One who makes widows by destroying husbands.

widow maker program – A CFA combat program specifically designed to teach the law abiding citizen how to use extreme force when faced with immediate threat of unlawful deadly criminal attack. The Widow Maker program is divided into two phases or methodologies: Webbing and Razing.

Y

yell—A loud and aggressive scream or shout used for various strategic reasons.

Z

zero beat – One of the four beat classifications of the Widow Maker, Feral Fighting and Savage Street Fighting Programs. Zero beat strikes are full pressure techniques applied to a specific target until it completely ruptures. They include gouging, crushing, biting, and choking techniques.

zone one—Anatomical targets related to your senses, including the eyes, temple, nose, chin, and back of neck.

zone three—Anatomical targets related to your mobility, including thighs, knees, shins, and instep.

zone two—Anatomical targets related to your breathing, including front of neck, solar plexus, ribs, and groin.

The 10 Best Ways to Develop Your Killer Instinct

About Sammy Franco

With over 30 years of experience, Sammy Franco is one of the world's foremost authorities on armed and unarmed self-defense. Highly regarded as a leading innovator in combat sciences, Mr. Franco was one of the premier pioneers in the field of "reality-based" self-defense and martial arts instruction.

Sammy Franco is perhaps best known as the founder and creator of Contemporary Fighting Arts (CFA), a state-of-the-art offensive-based combat system that is specifically designed for real-world self-defense. CFA is a sophisticated and practical system of self-defense, designed specifically to provide efficient and effective methods to avoid, defuse, confront, and neutralize both armed and unarmed attackers.

Sammy Franco has frequently been featured in martial art magazines, newspapers, and appeared on numerous radio and television programs. Mr. Franco has also authored numerous books, magazine articles, and editorials, and has developed a popular library of instructional videos.

Sammy Franco's experience and credibility in the combat sciences is unequaled. One of his many accomplishments in this field includes the fact that he has earned the ranking of a Law Enforcement Master Instructor, and has designed, implemented, and taught officer survival training to the United States Border Patrol (USBP). He has instructed members of the US Secret Service, Military Special Forces,

The 10 Best Ways to Develop Your Killer Instinct

Washington DC Police Department, Montgomery County, Maryland Deputy Sheriffs, and the US Library of Congress Police. Sammy Franco is also a member of the prestigious International Law Enforcement Educators and Trainers Association (ILEETA) as well as the American Society of Law Enforcement Trainers (ASLET) and he is listed in the "Who's Who Director of Law Enforcement Instructors."

Sammy Franco is a nationally certified Law Enforcement Instructor in the following curricula: PR-24 Side-Handle Baton, Police Arrest and Control Procedures, Police Personal Weapons Tactics, Police Power Handcuffing Methods, Police Oleoresin Capsicum Aerosol Training (OCAT), Police Weapon Retention and Disarming Methods, Police Edged Weapon Countermeasures and "Use of Force" Assessment and Response Methods.

Mr. Franco holds a Bachelor of Arts degree in Criminal Justice from the University of Maryland. He is a regularly featured speaker at a number of professional conferences and conducts dynamic and enlightening seminars on numerous aspects of self-defense and combat training.

On a personal level, Sammy Franco is an animal lover, who will go to great lengths to assist and rescue animals. Throughout the years, he's rescued everything from turkey vultures to goats. However, his most treasured moments are always spent with his beloved German Shepherd dogs.

For more information about Mr. Franco and his unique Contemporary Fighting Arts system, you can visit his website at: **SammyFranco.com** or follow him on twitter **@RealSammyFranco**

Other Books by Sammy Franco

KILLER INSTINCT
Unarmed Combat for Street Survival
by Sammy Franco

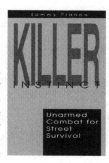

Here, Mr. Franco describes the mental, spiritual and physical components of his advanced system of combat that offers the fighter a brutal and efficient arsenal. But a weapon is only as good as the soldier trained to use it. Reading this book is the first step. Followed by proper and consistent training, the tools and techniques contained herein can be maximized by the martial artists who has attained self-knowledge, psychological preparedness and most importantly, mastery of the killer instinct. 8.5 x 5.5, paperback, photos, illus, 134 pages.

INVINCIBLE
Mental Toughness Techniques for Peak Performance
by Sammy Franco

Invincible is a treasure trove of battle-tested techniques and strategies for improving mental toughness in all aspects of life. It teaches you how to unlock the true power of your mind and achieve success in sports, fitness, high-risk professions, self-defense, and other peak performance activities. However, you don't have to be an athlete or warrior to benefit from this unique mental toughness book. In fact, the mental skills featured in this indispensable program can be used by anyone who wants to reach their full potential in life. 8.5 x 5.5, paperback, photos, illus, 250 pages.

WARRIOR WISDOM
Inspiring Ideas from the World's Greatest Warriors
by Sammy Franco

Warrior Wisdom includes a huge collection of unforgettable quotes, sayings and writings from warriors and warrior leaders, both past and present, and from around the world. This exhaustive book reveals the essentialities of the Fighter's life, speaking with great heart, eloquence, wisdom and an earned authenticity on subjects still crucial to you today: leadership, loyalty, honor, courage, tactics, strategy and much more. Warrior Wisdom offers a unique opportunity to thoroughly explore what it really means to be a warrior...in the worlds of yesterday and today! 7 x 10, paperback, 216 pages.

SAVAGE STREET FIGHTING
Tactical Savagery as a Last Resort
by Sammy Franco

In this revolutionary book, Sammy Franco reveals the science behind his most primal street fighting method. Savage Street Fighting is a brutal self-defense system specifically designed to teach the law-abiding citizen how to use "Tactical Savagery" when faced with the immediate threat of an unlawful deadly criminal attack. Savage Street Fighting is systematically engineered to protect you when there are no other self-defense options left! With over 300 photographs and detailed step-by-step instructions, Savage Street Fighting is a must-have book for anyone concerned about real world self-defense. Now is the time to learn how to unleash your inner beast! 8.5 x 5.5, paperback, 317 photos, illustrations, 232 pages.

FIRST STRIKE
End a Fight in Ten Seconds or Less!
by Sammy Franco

Learn how to stop any attack before it starts by mastering the art of the preemptive strike. First Strike gives you an easy-to-learn yet highly effective self-defense game plan for handling violent close-quarter combat encounters. First Strike will teach you instinctive, practical and realistic self-defense techniques that will drop any criminal attacker to the floor with one punishing blow. By reading this book and by practicing, you will learn the hard-hitting skills necessary to execute a punishing first strike and ultimately prevail in a self-defense situation. And that's what it is all about: winning in as little time as possible. 8.5 x 5.5, paperback, photos, illustrations, 202 pages.

WAR MACHINE
How to Transform Yourself Into A Vicious & Deadly Street Fighter
by Sammy Franco

War Machine is a book that will change you for the rest of your life! When followed accordingly, War Machine will forge your mind, body and spirit into iron. Once armed with the mental and physical attributes of the War Machine, you will become a strong and confident warrior that can handle just about anything that life may throw your way. In essence, War Machine is a way of life. Powerful, intense, and hard. 11 x 8.5, paperback, photos, illustrations, 210 pages.

KUBOTAN POWER
Quick and Simple Steps to Mastering the Kubotan Keychain
by Sammy Franco

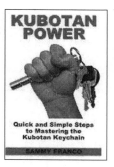

With over 290 photographs and step-by-step instructions, Kubotan Power is the authoritative resource for mastering this devastating self-defense weapon. In this one-of-a-kind book, world-renowned self-defense expert, Sammy Franco takes thirty years of real-world teaching experience and gives you quick, easy and practical kubotan techniques that can be used by civilians, law enforcement personnel, or military professionals. The Kubotan is an incredible self-defense weapon that has helped thousands of people effectively defend themselves. Men, women, law enforcement officers, military, and security professionals alike, appreciate this small and discreet self-defense tool. Unfortunately, however, very little has been written about the kubotan, leaving it shrouded in both mystery and ignorance. As a result, most people don't know how to unleash the full power of this unique personal defense weapon. 8.5 x 5.5, paperback, 290 photos, illustrations, 204 pages.

THE COMPLETE BODY OPPONENT BAG BOOK
by Sammy Franco

In this one-of-a-kind book, Sammy Franco teaches you the many hidden training features of the body opponent bag that will improve your fighting skills and boost your conditioning. With detailed photographs, step-by-step instructions, and dozens of unique workout routines, The Complete Body Opponent Bag Book is the authoritative resource for mastering this lifelike punching bag. The Complete Body Opponent Bag Book covers stances, punching, kicking, grappling techniques, mobility and footwork, targets, fighting ranges, training gear, time based workouts, punching and kicking combinations, weapons training, grappling drills, ground fighting, and dozens of workouts that will challenge you for years to come. 8.5 x 5.5, paperback, 139 photos, illustrations, 206 pages.

CONTEMPORARY FIGHTING ARTS
"Real World Self-Defense Since 1989"
SammyFranco.com

Made in the USA
Columbia, SC
17 December 2017